D0125395

LEARN TO
Love

make a success of your relationship

discover your emotional wisdom

develop respect, intimacy and passion

MARY JAKSCH

DUNCAN BAIRD PUBLISHERS

LONDON

For my son, Sebastian Grodd

Learn to Love
Mary Jaksch

First published in the United Kingdom and Ireland in 2001 by
Duncan Baird Publishers Ltd
Sixth Floor
Castle House
75–76 Wells Street
London W1T 3QH

Conceived, created and designed by Duncan Baird Publishers

Copyright © Duncan Baird Publishers 2001
Text copyright © Mary Jaksch 2001
Commissioned artwork copyright © Duncan Baird Publishers 2001

The right of Mary Jaksch to be identified as the Author of this
text has been asserted in accordance with the Copyright, Designs
and Patents Act of 1988.

All rights reserved. No part of this publication may be reproduced
or utilized in any form or by any means electronic or mechanical,
including photocopying, recording, or by any information storage
and retrieval system now known or hereafter invented, without
the prior written permission of the Publisher.

Managing Editor: Judy Barratt
Editor: Ingrid Court-Jones
Designed by: 27.12 Design Ltd., NYC
Commissioned Artwork: Anne Kristin Hagesæther

British Library Cataloguing-in-Publication Data:
A CIP record for this book is available from the British Library.

ISBN: 1-903296-46-3

10 9 8 7 6 5 4 3 2 1

Typeset in Bembo and Frutiger
Colour reproduction by Scanhouse, Malaysia
Printed by Imago, Singapore

NOTES
The abbreviations CE and BCE are used in this book:
CE Common Era (the equivalent of AD)
BCE Before the Common Era (the equivalent of BC)

contents

introduction

A loving relationship is a cornerstone of a joyful life. And yet many people suffer unhappiness and yearn for satisfying love. Maybe you sense some cracks in your relationship and want to heal your bond of love or maybe you are starting a new relationship and you fear repeating old patterns. Whatever your relationship is like, whether you are in a traditional marriage or another form of committed relationship, whether you love a person of the opposite or the same gender, there are principles at work that determine whether your relationship will increase or undermine your wellbeing. This book reveals these hidden principles and introduces step-by-step strategies to celebrate and enhance what is good in your relationship and to develop what is lacking. It will help you understand what your relationship needs in order to grow deep roots and flourish, by showing you how to achieve a balanced connection with your partner.

If you work through the book together, you and your partner will embark on a healing journey that can strengthen your relationship and bring back warmth, laughter and tenderness. However, if you prefer, you can also use this book on your own. When *you* change, everyone around you changes in response. You might also like to keep a relationship journal of your progress. You can then refer back to it at any time to track how far you have come on your journey and how much understanding you have gained along the way.

Chapter 1: The Relationship Recipe will help you to understand the ingredients of a good relationship. The guiding principle is love, with its components of passion, intimacy and commitment. If you read through these passages first, you will gain a clear sense of what is strong in your love and discover what needs to be developed. In this chapter, you will also explore the other key elements of a successful relationship: trust, empathy, truthfulness, kindness, respect and peacefulness.

Chapter 2: The Art of Positive Realism shows you how to look at your relationship in a new way. You will discover ways in which to draw on the emotional wisdom that lies hidden within you, and thus learn, for example, how to develop your trust through sexual love, how to experience the blessing of the present moment, and how to work through commonplace and difficult emotions, such as anger, jealousy and fear.

Chapter 3: Relationship Strategies teaches you how to improve your connections with each other, and offers ten step-by-step exercises to help you and your partner heal a flawed relationship. The very act of following a point-by-point strategy together, as you learn about giving and receiving love, will break down barriers and bring you closer together. You can either work through the strategies in sequence or, if you prefer, pick out the ones that seem most appropriate to the current circumstances in your relationship.

And finally, **Chapter 4: Widening the Network** shows you how to use your new skills and deeper understanding to enhance the relationships you have with people other than your loved one, such as family, friends and work colleagues.

the relationship recipe

Like cooking, a relationship needs the right ingredients in order to be successful. There is nothing prescriptive or classic about the recipe; there is lots of scope for individual variation. But there are basic principles of balance and flavouring, and tried-and-tested ways to make all the ingredients gel into a satisfying whole.

In this chapter you will find an all-purpose recipe for a good relationship. You will learn about the key factors that determine whether your relationship will bring you happiness or discord. You will also be equipped with a set of measuring spoons to assess the state of your relationship at this very moment. Love, with its aspects of passion, intimacy and commitment, is the main ingredient. But a relationship also needs trust, empathy, truthfulness, kindness, respect and peacefulness. Don't worry if you and your partner have differing views about the ideal relationship recipe: you will explore ways to work together for positive change. The exciting journey to a better relationship starts here.

love

"Like the stars over dark fields, love is the gift of eternal forces. We do not know why it appears; it is the song the universe sings to itself." As these words of Zen master John Tarrant imply, the human capacity for love is our greatest gift. The nineteenth-century French novelist Honoré de Balzac called love the poetry of the senses. At its most intense, love is the name we give to the sexual passion that is transfigured by emotion. Mutually felt, it binds two people like nothing else. Loss of that magical intensity is also enough to bring a relationship to an end, if we allow this to happen. But in a good relationship there are other aspects of love that underpin sexual desire and act as a source of mutual nourishment and inspiration, even through the most difficult times.

This is why, in any relationship, it can be helpful to explore and establish exactly what both you and your partner understand by "love". Dictionary definitions – "an intense feeling of deep affection or fondness for a person or thing" – don't get us very far. Two people can have different perceptions of love and express their responses in quite different ways. And while it is not necessary for our partner's idea of love to coincide with our own, we need to be clear about what our *expectations* of love are, as well as our partner's expectations. Otherwise, disappointment may lead to arguments that might appear trivial on the surface but in fact reflect deep-seated and dangerous disillusions.

Our ability to give and receive love as an adult is influenced by our experience of love in childhood. At one extreme are

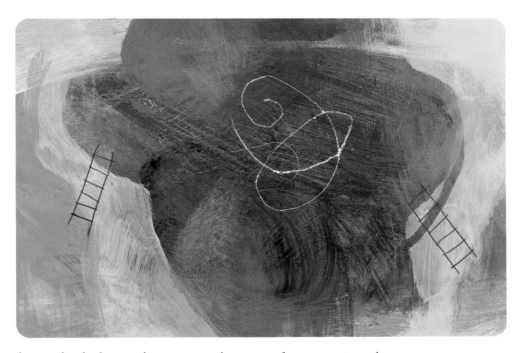

those who had great love, care and support from parents and other mentors and who experienced the emotional interplay of living with brothers, sisters or other close childhood friends. At the other are those who were unloved, lonely or, worse still, lived in fear of abuse. If you are setting out to improve an adult relationship, reflect for a moment on your own formative years. How do you think your childhood experiences may have determined your concept of love, your image of an ideal lover, and your idea of how to be lovable yourself?

It is important to understand how your attitude toward love was formed, but don't draw any conclusions now. Just try to keep your reflections in mind as you read on. The good news is that you can learn to love anew at any age!

If you think of all the people you cherish, you will know that you love each person in a unique way. You love a child differently from the way you love a parent or a friend. In the realm of sexual partnerships every bond is unique, but there are certain recognizable general patterns of love – a good basis from which we can begin to improve our relationship. The American psychologist Robert J. Sternberg has envisaged the main features of love as a series of interactions which form a triangle. The three points of the triangle he labels passion, intimacy and commitment. Love partnerships form different shapes of triangle, according to the weight given to each of these aspects in a relationship at any one time. Passion describes the ardent emotional and physical attraction, the powerful magnetism of touch. Intimacy covers other emotions such as loving friendship, sympathy and protectiveness. Commitment brings into play a wide range of factors that usually have more to do with the rational side of our nature and with the social, financial and cultural aspects of a stable relationship. These three basic components of love are explored in more depth on the following pages, but here is a taster to whet your appetite.

Passion adds excitement to a relationship. In the first heady days of being in love, your body's physical response to another human being can be so strong that it throws your emotional, sensual and mental faculties into turmoil. But passion can also be part of a later, more mature stage of love, resurfacing in sensual encounters that allow you to fall in love all over again.

If passion is characterized by the feeling of being "in love", then intimacy is the state of feeling "love for" someone. This dimension of love focuses on caring affection and openness. While passion can be like a white-hot flash at the beginning of a relationship, the pleasures of intimacy grow at a slow, gentle pace while you get to know each other. As intimacy develops, you begin to see each other as "real" people and feel a binding sympathy for each other's quirks – including imperfections.

Commitment means that you make a clear pledge of love and stick to it. Although most obviously expressed in living together or getting married, commitment can start with a simple decision to stop seeking out other partners. To commit yourself to loving someone is to accept boundaries to your own freedom. In a successful relationship, commitment is an active process, a resolve to address problems as they arise and nurture your bond of love. Its fruits are trust and security.

Love is the poetry of the senses. It is the key to all that is great in our destiny. It is sublime or it is nothing.

Honoré de Balzac
(1799–1850)

FOUR PATTERNS OF LOVE RELATIONSHIPS

Different levels of passion, intimacy and commitment in relationships produce a number of common patterns of love. High passion with low intimacy or commitment is characteristic of "romantic love". The relationship is probably still in its early stages with both partners feeling they are "in love". Fluctuating passion combined with the development of intimacy and commitment typifies a more stable relationship known as "mature love". When intimacy continues with little passion and commitment, the relationship is hardly more than friendship. This is characteristic of "open" relationships in which partners have a high degree of freedom. Where passion and intimacy are lost but commitment continues, the relationship has become "empty love".

passion

All thoughts, all passion,
all delights,
Whatever stirs this
mortal frame,
Are all but ministers
of Love,
And feed his
sacred flame.

Samuel Taylor Coleridge
(1772–1834)

Passion is state of mind, not an emotion; a driving force in us that *heightens* all emotions. Being driven by passion can be exhilarating but also frightening. When passion fuels jealousy and anger, it can lead to violence, even "crimes of passion". Brought to law, people who commit such crimes argue diminished responsibility – they were not their true selves but were "possessed" by extreme emotions. This is the realm of unhealthy passion. On the other hand, there can also be healthy passion, when the positive emotions that bring a couple together are intensified. When love and desire are driven by passion, a relationship is often long-lasting because the feelings a couple have for one another are so strong.

Passion most often manifests itself as a surge of sexual attraction. This surge involves some of the same chemical systems in our brain that operate when we face danger – the "flight or fight" response. The brain increases its production of the hormone epinephrine (adrenaline), preparing us to cope with a critical situation. And as passion wells inside us, the brain increases its production of endorphins, the chemical messengers that create a heightened sense of wellbeing.

When our passion is reciprocated by the person to whom we are attracted, we are drawn to touch and keep in close physical contact with them. Sexual attraction is especially strong when you start out in a relationship, but as your partnership matures, your passion will inevitably lose some of its early intensity. However, there's nothing untoward in this and in a healthy

relationship passion can be renewed at any time. One of the best ways is through sex (passion as erotic love is explored more fully on pp.50–51), but any activity that makes you feel "in love" or especially close to each other helps rekindle waning passion.

Passionate attraction can sometimes tip into unhealthy obsession, which is dangerous as it can lead to inner turbulence and

irresponsible behaviour. You know that you are obsessed when you cannot stop your thoughts circling around your object of desire, and when you show signs of compulsive behaviour. For example, are you cavalier about breaking your arrangements with others, including work commitments, in order to benefit from an unexpected chance to be with your loved one? Do you feel depressed when an anticipated meeting is cancelled for a legitimate reason? Are you often jealous? Do you feel possessive and attempt to control your partner's actions unreasonably?

Answering "yes" to any of these questions might make you suspect that your passionate desire for your loved one has turned into a love addiction. A desperate sense of ongoing panic and high levels of insecurity are symptomatic of love addiction. These can make you distracted at home and unfocused at work. You might become absent-minded or make careless mistakes. If any of this rings true for you, it may be important for you to spend some time alone to think about where you are going with this obsession. Sit comfortably in an armchair and extend your arms along the rests, your palms upward and your fingers curled loosely into fists. Give to one hand the voice of obsession and to the other the voice of reason. Now start a dialogue, uncurling the fingers to open each hand as it has its say. When both hands have "spoken", slowly clasp your hands together. Ask yourself what compromise there might be between reason and obsession. If you project your obsession into the future, and if the destination is not where you want to be, redraw the mental map you are following. If other relationships are being damaged, resolve that this will come to an end. Set yourself on a more even path.

Balancing passion with reason in this way might seem unromantic, but it is crucial if your relationship is to be long-lasting. The feelings that passion arouses will not continue at their early level of intensity. Successful relationships are all about balance. In an intimate and respectful relationship, passion is a gift that keeps your desire for each other alive. A balance of passion and friendship is a perfect recipe for long-term harmony.

Now use the box below to try to assess how your relationship fares on the "passion scale".

THE PASSION INDICATOR

This passion indicator will help you and your partner determine the level and kind of passion in your relationship.

The scores are:
1 = never, 2 = rarely, 3 = sometimes, 4 = often, 5 = constantly.

- Do you miss your partner when you are apart?
- Do you feel a sense of excitement in your relationship?
- Do you want to touch and cuddle your partner at all times?
- Do you fear that you might lose your partner?
- Do you feel elated when you are with your partner?
- Does your anxiety level rise when you are with your partner?
- Are you sexually aroused by your partner outside the bedroom?

A score between 1 and 11 signifies a low level of passion. Think about rekindling the passion that lies at the heart of your love. A score between 12 and 23 shows that passion is of medium intensity in your relationship. This means that your relationship has matured. A high score of between 24 and 35 shows that you are still "in love". You need to develop intimacy so that your love can flourish and endure.

intimacy

The only gift is a portion of thyself.

Ralph Waldo Emerson
(1803–1882)

What do you understand by the term "intimacy"? Focus on non-sexual intimacy for now and note down the five most intimate moments you can remember experiencing with your partner. Most likely, these will be shared moments of deep affection or "connectedness". For example, perhaps you felt especially intimate when you and your partner both tried to telephone each other at exactly the same time, as if by telepathy; or when you looked across a crowded room into each other's eyes; or when you shared with each other a secret thought expressed in a coded glance. When you have finished your list, put it aside – we will come back to it shortly.

If you have been together for many years, you might feel that intimacy has waned in your relationship. Instead of feeling connected, you might even sometimes feel lonely in each other's company. This experience is often saddening and confusing – in the course of everyday living we may well spend a lot of time together (share chores, watch TV together, sleep together, and so on), so we find it hard to work out how intimacy can have been lost. The answer is simple: we get immersed in the humdrum routine of living together and begin to take each other for granted. On top of this, we can get so bogged down with stress that our thoughts continually revolve around our worries about work, or money, or how the children are doing. It is as if we live in a fog of anxiety, which disconnects us from our partner.

If any of this rings true for you, take heart because there are ways of overcoming this separateness. When we are preoccupied,

we are not really *present* with our partner. We need to stop what we are doing or thinking and consciously re-establish an intimate connection. The key to doing this is through awareness. When we become intensely aware of each other again, our feeling of intimacy increases.

Think back to your list of five intimate moments in your partnership. What made them intimate? We have mentioned feelings of "affection" and "connectedness". What other emotions might be cited? Perhaps a moment was intimate because you felt it held a shared experience; or because you felt valued; or because there was an exceptional openness between the two of you; or because you felt a sense of physical and emotional ease. Think about your relationship as it is now – how often do you experience

intimacy? How often are you truly and wholly aware of your partner? Use the exercise on the opposite page to assess the true level of intimacy in your relationship.

There are some intimate moments in our relationship that we come to expect. As a result, we may not consciously notice them, or we may take them for granted. We can be undressed together without inhibition. We can sit together in a room and feel not the slightest sense that we have to be anyone other than ourselves, or that we would feel more comfortable alone.

Such is the intimacy between established partners that there will be few taboo subjects for conversation – only perhaps a reticence to raise topics that might cause emotional ripples. However, avoid the pitfall of automatism – an intimacy taken so much for granted that no courtesy, no real communication, and no special consideration of each other's feelings are deemed necessary. You may have noticed, perhaps with discomfort, other couples behaving toward each other in ways you might perceive as off-hand or sullen. Ask yourself if there is scope in your own relationship for improving your manners toward your partner, for being more generous and thoughtful in your courtesies, for sending out a signal of appreciation now and then.

Not saying "please" or "thank you", or saying them in a hasty, mumbled manner without a smile; not wishing each other good morning or good night; expressing your thoughts, not in clear considerate language but in a series of non-verbal noises and gestures – all these are symptoms that your intimacy may need an injection of effort on your part, or by both of you, to endow it with a due sense of cherishing and being cherished.

exercise 1

THE INTIMACY BAROMETER

The Intimacy Barometer shows the level of closeness in your relationship.
Complete the exercise individually, but concurrently. Monitor your
behaviour in this way at the end of every week, for 6 weeks.

one
Make twelve photocopies of this page – two for each week. At the end of each week,
take some quiet time together and assess the statements independently, giving each
answer a score of between 1 and 5. Then each record your total score.
The scores: **1** = never, **2** = rarely, **3** = sometimes, **4** = often, **5** = constantly

This week you:
- *showed kindness toward me*
- *helped me with something*
- *disclosed thoughts and feelings*
- *shared activities with me*
- *spent time talking with me*
- *laughed with me*
- *showed tenderness toward me*

This week I:
- *felt relaxed and at ease with you*
- *felt close to you*
- *enjoyed hugging you*
- *valued what is different about you*
- *experienced companionship with you*

two
Exchange pages and read your partner's scores. Do not comment, but thank your partner.
Then, discuss how you might both be able to show more intimacy toward one another.
Where are there areas of low score? What effort can each of you make to work on these
areas? Perhaps one of you feels that something had an unjustly low score – talk about
why. Might one of you have unwittingly taken something the other did for granted?

commitment

Our commitment to each other is a bed of well-tilled soil in which our bond grows strong and true. Without pledging our time and support to each other, and avowing some kind of long-term intention (however experimental), love is likely either to perish or to bring us heartache. In a successful relationship we must be prepared to translate good feelings into sustained effort. We must surrender some of our individual options in life, hoping that we will be rewarded by mutual fulfilment. Then, when difficulties arise, we are able to take a long-term view of our relationship and put each problem into perspective against the backdrop of a shared life that is filled with trust, safety and openness.

Ideally, commitment is a conscious process but some people drift into the life choices they make. They find themselves tied to responsibilities but have no distinct memory of committing to a certain vision of the future. How did I end up here?, they might ask. This slide into commitment can lead to resentment and a feeling of being trapped.

A more satisfying approach is to move along the stages of commitment at your own pace and with full awareness of all the implications. There are distinct landmarks on the commitment journey. For example, the moment you decide to be true to each other and not pursue any potential new partners is an early milestone. Telling any secrets in your past can be an important step. Living together is an obvious watershed, but long before that you might choose to start behaving as a recognizable couple –

sharing vacations, even helping each other with family responsibilities. Other major stages might include a pooling of financial resources and, of course, marriage and having children.

Looked at like this, commitment sounds like a progression of natural steps. So why is the word for many so charged with anxiety? Some people may fear that commitment means becoming trapped in a relationship, because it seems so final. Some may fear that they will be exploited financially. Often such fears stem from difficult past relationships or from a general sense of mistrust. Share any such anxieties with your partner. Set a realistic relationship timetable. Be open about your individual goals. Be patient. And be ready to move on if your partner seems likely to postpone indefinitely the crucial next step you long to take.

I am yours,
You are mine.
Of this we are certain.
You are lodged in my
heart, the small
key is lost.
You must stay
there forever.

Frau Ava (12th century)

trust

Trust is a double act: it involves a willingness on the one side to be dependable, on the other side to be dependent. An extreme example is a pair of circus artists high on a trapeze. One is the catcher, the other the flyer. Before the flyer entrusts her life (I say "her" only to avoid a crowd of pronouns) to the catcher, she has to ask herself some important questions: is the catcher a good person, who will not intentionally cause me harm? Is he reliable and focused – will he be ready to catch me at the crucial moment? Is he competent – does he have the skills and the strength to catch me? The flyer would want to be assured that the answers to these questions are a resounding "yes" before she would even consider letting go of the bar! Then comes the moment of absolute dependency, of vulnerability, when the flyer lets go and throws herself into the catcher's hands.

Trust is a feeling that needs to be built up in a relationship – the flyer would not be able to assess the catcher's goodness, reliability and competence if she had only just met him. The longer we are together, the more we learn about our partner and the more we feel that we can trust them (or not, as the case may be). Trust is a retrospective principle that looks back over the track-record. This is why it is so important that we take our responsibility seriously: a blot on our copybook can be difficult to expunge, and for the sake of one act out of character our relationship might suffer enormously, whether that act was selfish, careless, well-intentioned, blundering or deliberately deceptive. Of course, there is a scale of significance, and forgetting to buy

mineral water at the store despite the reminder you were given as you left home is hardly the same as letting down your team-mate in a circus show. Forgetting to call at a pharmacy for pre-scription drugs might be a different matter. Either of these failures could no doubt be easily rectified, but they bring in their wake two distinct problems. First, at the practical level, how can the relationship run smoothly if one partner shows that he or she is prone to letting down the other? Once the track-record starts to look less than glowing, imagine the anxiety that accompanies any request for an errand to be done. Secondly, there is a sym-bolism at work here: the problem with breaking your partner's trust is that it might be perceived as lack of consideration.

Forgetfulness is not necessarily a mental aberration: it can also be interpreted as a preoccupation with one's own concerns, a self-ishness, a lack of regard for the other. In sum, the effort you put into justifying the trust invested in you, even in relatively unim-portant matters, is one of the keys to a healthy relationship.

If you live together, many issues of household management will reflect badly on both of you if they are handled in an irre-sponsible manner. For example, if your partner takes responsibil-ity for certain household bills yet fails to pay them on time, that is a breach of trust. Of course, there is a whole range of much weightier issues that fall under the rubric of trust – in particular, fidelity and, in a broader sense, the honouring of a declared com-mitment to take the relationship further. Health can play a part in this too, on a whole range of issues, from promising and fail-ing to see a doctor, to making a genuine attempt to conquer an addiction. On such serious matters, trust starts to loom large in conversation. Promises are required and given, raising the signif-icance of trust to an even higher level. To break a promise is self-destructive: better not to promise anything in the first place if you believe that you might not be able to deliver a satisfactory outcome; better to promise merely to *try*.

A related but often overlooked cause for concern is unjustified *mis*trust. An example would be one person having difficulty accepting that the other really loved him or her – possibly because of low self-esteem. This is a situation where a plea for trust can be more effective than an attempted proof. Love is subject to neither proof nor disproof, so trust is in fact a vital component of love.

We often speak of earning someone's trust, which is a good way of putting it, because it underlines the fact that trust is a very precious aspect of a loving relationship. If our partner trusts us absolutely, this is a gift beyond measure – they have placed an important part of themselves within our care, and if we really wish to show commitment within the relationship we must take every possible step to treat that privilege responsibly and lovingly.

A SMALL ADVENTURE OF SURRENDER

When our ability to trust has been broken – whether in childhood or adulthood – mending it can be a long process. Try the following exercise, which helps rebuild your confidence in your partner without the need to discuss your relationship. If ever you require reassurance that your partner has your wellbeing at heart, do the exercise again. All you will need for it are a blindfold and a scarf.

Put on the blindfold and then ask your partner to tie your hands loosely behind your back using the scarf. Then, your partner should put his or her right arm around your waist and hold your left arm with his or her left hand. For the next 5 minutes they should guide you on a tour around your home (in silence, by whatever route they please), leading you from room to room, around furniture, through doorways, up steps, around the garden or backyard. Afterwards, sit down together and discuss how it felt for you to place all your faith in your partner. Ask your partner how it felt to be trusted so completely. When you feel ready, repeat the exercise in a local park – how does this feel different? Does it require more or less trust in your partner? Then, try the exercise with your partner blindfold and you leading. Discuss how he or she felt and how this tallies with or differs from your experience.

empathy

The ability to identify completely with the feelings of the other person, without becoming consumed by them, is a vital ingredient in a successful relationship. This is empathy. It is a matter not just of understanding, but of a shared response. How can you be happy together if you are unable or unwilling to feel *with* your partner – to have a vivid sense of their emotions?

There are three main steps to empathizing with someone: recognizing the person's emotions for what they are; stepping into the other's shoes so that you fully understand where the emotions have sprung from; and identifying with the emotions – even to the extent of feeling them yourself – so that you respond appropriately. The eighteenth-century philosopher Adam Smith outlined these three steps beautifully in his work *The Theory of Moral Sentiments*. He described recognizing emotions as bringing "a case home to one's own bosom"; stepping into the shoes of another as "trading places in fancy"; and feeling their emotion as "beating time with their heart".

Empathy begins with a highly sensitive reading of others' emotions. However, these emotions are often coded in our body language and don't usually announce themselves in straightforward terms. With practice we can train ourselves to notice the way in which our partner's emotions present themselves simply by paying closer attention. For example, when he or she comes home from work try to gauge the kind of day they have had from their posture and their manner. If they had a difficult day, their shoulders may droop and they may have an air of defeat

about them; if they had a productive day they may stand tall (and walk with confident strides) and they may also seem more animated than usual. If we can pick up on these signs and respond empathetically, our partner will feel understood and cherished.

Your ability to empathize with your partner is also increased if you can share your emotions verbally with each other. For example, ask your partner to use metaphors or similes such as "I feel as if I'm hollow inside"; or "I feel as if I could conquer the world." Using expressive language to convey your emotions precisely, rather than stating blandly, say, "I feel sad" or "I am angry", makes it easier for your partner to step into your shoes.

Empathy is an act of imagination and will occur only if you keep your imagination engaged. Spend a few minutes examining whether you are currently successful in this respect. Do you take decisions without considering how they will affect your partner? Do you put him or her down in front of others? Try to remember the last time you were inconsiderate toward your partner and imagine how you would feel if the roles were reversed.

It is more difficult to empathize with predicaments that are alien to your own character or experiences. Let's say, for example, that your partner has had a dreadful month at work – he or she has had to work late every night and at weekends, struggling against a growing workload, with negligible support from colleagues. You, on the other hand, are in a job that requires very different skills, have had an enjoyable time, in a sympathetic environment. Your partner comes home one evening and breaks down. He or she tries to explain, but the scenario is not something that you can readily connect with. In this case, empathy manifests itself as an active concern to understand more about the crisis, and to help as appropriate. The situation might take a lot of explaining. But by listening patiently and caringly you can enter the realm that is so alien to you – like a hero in a myth entering the Underworld to rescue one of the demon's victims.

When we truly allow ourselves to be touched by the emotions of another human being and make an effort to understand what they might be experiencing, we move from empathy to its crowning glory – compassion: an open-hearted, positive, constructive involvement in another's predicament. For more on compassion turn to the Strategies chapter (pp.102–5).

exercise 2

LOOKING THROUGH THE CRYSTAL WINDOW

This simple exercise will allow you and your partner to gain a clearer insight into each other's thought processes. It can help you to develop your skills of recognizing your partner's emotions. And, in difficult times, it can be a useful way to reassure one another that you are trying to understand each other's feelings.

one
Choose a time when you are both relaxed and a place where you can work together undisturbed. Focus on the empathy you already have for your partner. Think about how your partner has been feeling recently, and imagine standing alongside them in those feelings, appreciating and even experiencing them yourself.

two
Now take time to observe your partner's body and face to find clues to their inner feelings. A hunched posture indicates resignation or sorrow, whereas an upright posture speaks of confidence. Do their eyes look sad or anxious? Look at how they hold their mouth – it will tell you whether they are, say, happy, disapproving, sad or angry. Are their hands clenched in anger or are they fidgeting with worry? You may find it difficult to notice subtle changes in your partner's face and body when you do this exercise for the first time, but you will become more observant with practice.

three
Now gently offer your observations to your partner. You might say, "I notice that your hands are clenched and I wonder whether you are feeling frustrated or angry." Each time you comment, invite your partner to correct or confirm your guess. As you continue you will become more and more absorbed in the situation, you will become more sensitive and astute, and you may feel strong emotions well up.

four
When you have each had a turn at observing, share your experience with your partner. Afterwards, do something relaxing and enjoyable to refresh yourselves both emotionally and mentally.

truthfulness

Love is patient;
love is kind;
love is not envious or
boastful or arrogant
or rude. It does not
insist on its own way;
it is not irritable or
resentful; it does not
rejoice in wrongdoing,
but rejoices in
the truth.

1 Corinthians 13:4–6

Before we begin to look into the role of truthfulness in our relationship, we should spend a little time thinking about the terminology. Being "truthful" is different from, but at the same time a fundamental part of, being "true". It is important in our search for spiritual meaning, and to the fundamental questions we ask ourselves in that search: where have I come from? Where am I going? What is my purpose in life?

If we are true, we act in a way that we know instinctively to be right. This means, among other things, that we are honest. Most moral codes demand honesty. That is because harmony among people is disturbed through lying. We are happiest when we follow our natural inclination to believe, and believe in, those whom we love. And when our trust in what these people say and imply is betrayed, this strikes right to the core of our being. Consider also the effect that dishonesty has on the perpetrator: when you lie there is a part of you that feels shame and guilt. These unpleasant feelings often result in a wish to withdraw or separate yourself from the person you have wronged, as their presence reminds you continually of your transgression. If you have been unfaithful, or for any other reason are tangled in a web of lies, you will begin to feel more and more distant from your partner. It is as if love demands that you bring all of yourself into the relationship. If you withhold a part of yourself, love tends to wither. If you lie or distort the truth when communicating with your partner, you are failing your true self – your integrity – as well as failing this person's trust in you.

With strangers or mere acquaintances truthfulness remains a moral issue, but a less critical one. We all know people who tend to be guarded with strangers, especially when talking of personal matters. There are many reasons for behaving like this, ranging from modesty or shyness to a belief that one's personal life, especially those areas of it that are shared with a partner, are not for public consumption. It is all a matter of temperament.

Even those of us who are outgoing in character often show a tendency to wear "masks" in our relations with others, so as to seem more likeable or more impressive. Some people wear the "nice person" mask, with a smile pasted on, saying everything is

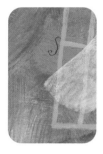

always "fine", even though there is turbulence under-neath. Then there's the "strong person", who is always in control, never cries, is always efficient and cool under fire — while underneath is an anxious person with low self-esteem. There's a whole dressing-up box full of other possibilities — the party-lover, the serious person with no time for play, the juggler who can meet any emotional demand. Do the exercise opposite to find out more about your real selves: you'll find it scary but fascinating.

If we can choose to be truthful in everything we do or say to each other, our relationship will be founded in realism, each partner fully knowing the other. I said "everything we say or do", but actually many of us have secrets, even from those closest to us. Often these are in closed areas of the past, and there is no need to feel that such dark corners have to be laid bare: it can do more harm than good, because it raises the question, Why tell me this now? However, secrets that are live — such as an undeclared close friendship with romantic overtones — are certainly against the spirit of a loving, trustful relationship.

That is not to say that any mask you wear with your partner is adopted with ignoble intentions. You might conceal the hurt a relative has done you because you know that your partner has worse family problems of their own, or you fear being boring on the subject. Even in such a case it is usually best to be truthful, although without demanding too much attention or sympathy.

The truth will be painful at times. If you find yourself hearing uncomfortable insights about yourself, accept them for what they are. Value your partner's courage and honesty in speaking them.

exercise 3

PEELING AWAY THE MASKS

In our daily lives we often wear "masks" which reveal only certain sides of ourselves, obscuring our true nature. To make your relationship work, you have to do away with masks and reveal your true self to your partner. As you do the following exercise, be sure to give each other plenty of emotional support. You will need some large sheets of plain, thick paper, some coloured pencils, some string, a pair of scissors and some adhesive tape.

one
Sitting comfortably together, each spend 2 or 3 minutes deciding which of your daily "masks" you most often wear for your partner. Perhaps it is that of the carer or confidante, which really hides a frustrated or needy part of you. Try to imagine what this mask would look like if you could walk into a store and buy it.

two
Now take the coloured pencils and each draw your personal mask, life-size, on a sheet of thick paper or thin cardboard. Don't worry about being artistic – just do the best you can. Cut out the eyes of your mask. Attach two bits of string when you have finished, to secure it to your face. Don't worry if you find yourselves giggling – laughter will help to keep the mood light and positive.

three
Decide who will put on their mask first. This person ties on their mask and speaks as this aspect of themselves. For example, if your mask is that of the carer, you might talk about the fact that you feel unable to ask for help yourself. Take off your mask and verbally list five emotions or characteristics that wearing the mask does not let you reveal in day-to-day life. Discuss how and why you hide your true self behind this persona. How can your partner help you to lose the mask for ever?

four
When you have both had a turn in your masks, spend 5 minutes each saying what you love best about the other. Then discuss any points raised that you feel do not reflect the true you – at least not all of the time. How might your partner have misunderstood you and why? End the session with a warm embrace.

kindness

Kindness is closely linked with happiness: the kinder you are to others, the happier you will be. This is the law of karma, of just returns. Sharon Salzberg, a teacher of the Buddhist "loving-kindness" meditation, has described kindness as the ability to embrace warmly all parts of ourselves, as well as all parts of the world. Really, kindness is the greatest of human arts, and as you practise it your heart becomes more open, infused by a sense of happiness and peace.

In fact, kindness is a natural instinct, shown even by primates, our "cousins" in the animal kingdom, in grooming and feeding each other. But humans, as they age, can lose touch with this impulse, their hearts contracting around painful experiences of fear, hurt and disappointment.

To trace how kindness happens, think of yourself taking a kindly initiative in a line to the supermarket checkout – perhaps allowing an elderly person to go ahead of you. You exchange smiles and feel a shaft of contented connection pass through you as your own preoccupations recede for a few moments. Your action was spontaneous: there was no thought of being "good" or "kind", only a natural flow. To be kind in this way depends on noticing other people and what their needs are. You responded, moreover, in a spirit of friendliness. These are all core aspects of kindness. The barriers to kindness, on the other hand, are selfishness, self-absorption, resentment and fear.

Now, having read my account of being kind toward a stranger, look closely at how you behave with your partner. Are you kind

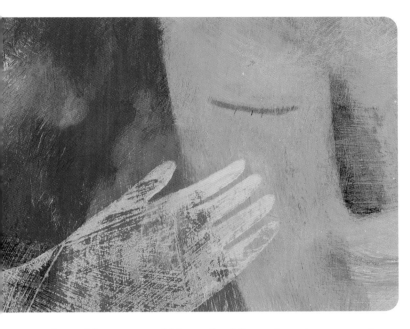

and considerate toward him or her? Sometimes it seems easier to
be kind to people we don't know than to the one we love. Why
is this? Perhaps we tend to take the person closest to us for
granted; perhaps we are unobservant; perhaps we walk through
our relationship in a fog of preoccupation that prevents us from
responding to our partner's needs; or perhaps we simply feel that
kindness is not part of the mutually agreed repertoire of suitable
responses in our lives. If the latter applies to your relationship,
you are trapped in a self-perpetuating shortfall in realizing your
true potential, but you can remedy this shortfall by taking
unilateral action.

Sometimes we store up resentment from past hurts in a way
that prevents us from being kind and open toward our loved one
– we want to be kind and yet we let slip hurtful little digs and

barbed remarks. And at times frustration from other parts of our life spills over into our relationship and we become unkind or even a little vicious. If any of this rings true for you, make a conscious decision now to change the way you relate to your partner and learn the art of kindness. You need to develop an involved, alert, considerate approach to your partner and you need to be *more fully present* in your relationship.

Without kindness there can be no true joy.

Thomas Carlyle
(1795–1881)

There is a simple way to practise this idea of being fully present. Train yourself to look at your partner more often than you currently do, and take a deep, slow breath as you do so. Still the chatter of your inner thoughts. When he or she talks to you, take your eyes away from your newspaper or TV program or whatever it is you have been concentrating on, breathe deeply and slowly, and give your partner real, mindful attention. Imagine that your mind is filled with clouds. These part to reveal a clear sky – empty space in which to give due attention.

Think of kindness as a natural way of being. Remember the way we say, "Would you be so kind as to … ?" In this courteous phrase we indicate that kindness is instinctive human behaviour, that it is part of our language, that it needs no emphasis to be understood. Make it such in your own lives together.

What if you feel that you are receiving more kindness than you are giving? Well, if this bothers you, there might indeed be an issue you should raise with your partner. But, if possible, try not to get hung up on such comparisons. Qualities like kindness cannot be quantified, so there is no point in trying to determine whether you have equality. The true spirit of kindness is to give without counting the cost.

exercise 4

THE SECRET GIFT

In this exercise you will perform conscious acts of kindness toward your partner. However, the real benefit will be for you. Each time you are considerate and kind, your heart will open up just a little more, and you will probably feel lighter and happier. The exercise has two parts, to be performed in parallel with each other. The first part involves secret acts of kindness – secret so that you can be sure that your motives are pure. The second part focuses on a new attitude you might try whenever there is a disagreement between you. Both exercises are ways of presenting secret gifts to your partner. Of course, you can try each part independently of the other if you wish.

one
At least three times per week find an opportunity to be kind to your partner without him or her being aware of your intention. For example, perhaps you might search hard to find something your partner has mislaid and then put the item in a place where they are sure to see it – to give them the satisfaction of discovery. Or, you might secretly forgo an evening out with friends in order to surprise your partner with tickets for a new movie they are keen to see. The common element in these two examples is that in neither case do you draw attention to your own virtue or achievement.

two
Each time you feel frustration or anger rising up in you in response to something your partner says (or does), make a conscious effort to practise "loving kindness". The natural reaction in a quarrel is to bluster, counterattack or cringe. But next time you are in heated disagreement, try something new. Stay calm, and resist the impulse to advance in attack or retreat in panic. Breathe deeply, and make a conscious effort to acknowledge but not follow your emotions. Now appreciate, in a spirit of kindness, that what your partner is saying is genuinely how he or she experiences the situation. All through the argument, focus on what you have in common, not on your differences. Keep your voice low and steady, your body movements slow. Let all the cutting remarks you might have made go unspoken. Instead, ask each other constructive questions, such as, "What would make this better for you?" or "What should we do differently next time?"

respect

No matter how much love there is in your relationship, treating each other with disrespect is inevitably a road to unhappiness. On the other hand, an underpinning of respect allows love to grow and flourish. Respect is an acknowledgment of positive qualities, a well-intentioned wish to allow those qualities their rightful significance in the way we regard each other and behave toward each other.

A necessary basis for respect is the way in which you treat your own self. If you have low self-esteem, true respect for another is difficult to muster, because you are always going to be making an inner comparison between yourself and the other person, possibly with a tinge of envy. You might even find yourself reacting against the positive qualities your partner shows by belittling them in some way – either openly or just in your own mind. A healthy sense of self-worth, however, gives you a clear perspective in which to appreciate your partner's merits without being affected by any emotional backwash. You simply admire this person, and your admiration becomes an inextricable part of your love.

One common form of behaviour that runs counter to respect is the put-down, by which one partner tries to make the other feel smaller. Put-downs are difficult to deal with because they often come out of the blue in the presence of other people, who then witness an embarrassing skirmish if you should choose to counterattack. Furthermore, they often take the form of a joke, which gives them a defensive shield: if you get angry or upset,

you will sometimes hear, "Oh, can't you even take a joke?" – thereby adding a further level of injury against you. It is worth stating unambiguously that put-downs are not an acceptable part of dialogue between people who love each other: indeed, the put-down is not a dialogue at all, and reflects badly on the per-petrator. Such aberrations are best dealt with firmly. You might try saying, in a reasonable tone of voice, "That put-down hurts. Please excuse me now," then leaving, wherever you are. It is not unreasonable to do this even when friends are there to witness the scene, as the message that this is intolerable will then be driven home. But in this or other situations, you might choose instead to save your comments until you and your partner are

alone together. Be absolutely clear that the boundary of accept-able behaviour has been crossed, and that you will not tolerate this again. Teasing, though related, is usually distinguished easily from a put-down, and if you do not enjoy being teased (many people do), you can make your point in a milder fashion.

Developing respect for a partner means focusing on what is good in their character or achievements. It is possible to spend time deploring this or that habit or aspect of personality: nobody is so perfect that they are immune from this kind of criticism. But it is much healthier to concentrate on the positive. You might feel that the ideals you attributed to your partner in the first flush of love are starting to peel off. Or perhaps you find that one of the characteristics that originally attracted you has in time become irritating in some way: to take an extreme case, people who fall for geniuses often find out very soon that the great person is maddeningly self-absorbed. To gain a fresh perspective, ask yourself what are the gifts that your partner's difference from yourself brings into your life. This question is especially interesting and important when you apply it to the character traits you find most difficult to handle.

If your partner's culture, ethnicity or religion is different from your own, one way to show and maintain respect is to learn as much as possible about their heritage. Think of your relationship as enriched by this cultural fusion. And remember that your difference from them is as significant as theirs from you. One of you might belong to a minority of nationality, race or belief in the area or country where you live, and minorities can be conspicuous. But standing out in some way need not detract from a person's sense of self. You are still defined by your own individuality and background no less than by your choice of partner.

Finally, we need to look at the way in which respect can be threatened by human error. Imagine that you respect your partner's professional skills as a financial adviser but that one day he or she causes their client to lose a great deal of money on the stockmarket because for once their analysis of economic trends is misguided. Do they forfeit any of your respect? The answer has to be that anyone is allowed to make mistakes, that this field of endeavour is all about risk, and that you are not qualified to say that the risk in this case was unacceptable. Do not forget, in any case, that this person you love now needs your empathy and support more than ever. Do not withhold your respect unless you are absolutely forced to do so.

THE INVENTORY OF TREASURES

In order to nurture self-respect – the necessary basis for respecting others – you need to identify and value your good points or "treasures". In your diary, write down each week the occasions when your good points triumphed. If you hear your "gremlin" (that is, your negative self-belief) whispering critical remarks into your ear, flick this destructive creature off your shoulder!

Note down the moments when your partner's qualities shine through and remember that their character traits and skills are your treasures also. Keep a record – or celebrate inwardly if you are not a great diarist – every time you see these qualities working on your behalf. Congratulate your partner for every display of good quality: make them aware of your appreciation.

peacefulness

Peace is something we find both in nature and at home when we manage to escape the demands and stresses of everyday, modern life. Ideally, a relationship should also offer a refuge and form a bulwark against all the pressures, such as work, social and financial demands, from the outside world.

All too often, however, life at home is far from peaceful, especially when you have children or other relatives living with you. You find yourself constantly under pressure to respond to their demands, as well as trying to meet those of your partner. It is hardly surprising then, that many of us recognize peacefulness as a highly desirable, indeed necessary, ingredient in our lives. Peacefulness is associated with contentment, freedom from stress, freedom from interference. It is the mood in which we meditate and in which, through meditation, we glimpse our true selves. So how do we bring peacefulness into our lives together? And what exactly does the term mean?

The first thing to say is that peacefulness is a quality found within the self rather than in external circumstances. This is good news, as it means that even a home shared with two or three young children, including a baby who cries some nights, can be a place of peace. The secret of finding peace is to go with the flow of life rather than against it. This involves patience, acceptance, a sense of the basic pointlessness of attempting to exert our will on circumstances beyond our control. It also involves appreciating our blessings much more feelingly than we recognize our misfortunes. As with all true arts, we need to practise finding

peace in order to improve our ability to discover it. But the magic is this: that peacefulness is contagious! You can start a peace movement within your own four walls, and it will spread in ever-widening circles, touching all those around you.

The second thing to say is that peacefulness means staying grounded within the core of your being and, at the same time, adapting to changes. If we are flexible in our thoughts and actions, we will be able to weather the storms in our relationship. The bamboo is a wonderful image of such flexibility, borrowed from Eastern thought. When a typhoon rages, the bamboo bends over; but as soon as the storm abates, it springs back upright again. If you are flexible in your thoughts and actions, you

We find rest in those we love, and we provide a resting place in ourselves for those who love us.

St Bernard of Clairvaux (1090–1153)

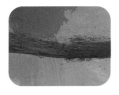

cannot be damaged so easily. You will find it much easier to attain peace. Adapting to change means to learn from what is new or difficult. When we are open to learning, we are being flexible; we are going with the flow instead of trying to swim upstream. Take time to think about a difficult situation you encountered in your relationship recently and ask yourself, "What can I learn from this?"

Acceptance leads to more peacefulness in a relationship because it reduces friction. One of the things you cannot change is your partner's personality – although you can inspire good habits by example or by encouragement. If you try to change the unchangeable (like trying to halt the march of time), you inevitably fail in the attempt and in consequence of your failure become deeply frustrated. (Really, there is nothing more frustrating than exerting our will to absolutely no avail.)

An enemy of peace is impatience. Whenever your relationship is in transition – for example, when you and your partner are on the step-by-step journey toward commitment, or in the process of moving toward agreeing on a shared vision of the future – it is important to allow things to happen at a pace that may well be much slower than you desire. If your wishes, like wild horses, are galloping away with you, the only satisfactory response is to slow

down. Breathe deeply and calmly, and reflect on the fact that different aspects of life have their own gestation periods and vary also from one individual to another. Love itself can happen in a moment, or over a period of weeks or months, or even years. Give yourselves peace by allowing every development in your partnership its natural rhythm of growth.

exercise 5

PEACEFUL TIME OUT

A wonderful way to develop peacefulness in your own heart and within your relationship is to spend quiet time together, perhaps filled with either meditation or prayer. Here is a simple but effective way to meditate together. Try to do the exercise at least once a week. It makes an excellent way to start the Heart Hour that is described in the Time Strategy (p.125). You will need a clock to time the exercise, which should last for about 10 minutes.

one
Choose a peaceful room where you will not be interrupted and a time when you feel reasonably wakeful. Place the clock where you can see it, so that you can time yourselves.

two
Sit side by side. Make sure that your posture is upright – sit either in a chair that supports your back, or on cushions on the floor, and push your breastbone out to straighten your back. Rest your hands on your thighs, the left hand nestling in the right, thumb-tips lightly touching.

three
Keeping your head upright, let your steady gaze sink down to the floor. Now focus your awareness on your body. Be aware of the pressure on your buttocks from the chair or cushions, your forearms resting on your thighs, your shoulders losing their tension.

four
Focus on your breath flowing in and out. Let that be the anchor that keeps you in the present moment. Open your awareness to sounds around you and let them flow right through you. When thoughts take you away from the present, gently let them go and focus on your breath again. Let them drift away like clouds. Just be.

five
At the end of the exercise, face your partner, bow your head slightly, and put your palms together in a gesture of love and respect. Appreciate him or her as a fellow pilgrim on the path to peacefulness.

the art
of positive realism

To be positive means using the power of hope to effect change. And being a realist entails living life as it really is, facing the difficulties as well as fully enjoying the valuable ingredients of your love bond. Joined together they make up the art of positive realism.

In this chapter you learn how to set and achieve realistic goals in your relationship; how to live in the present, so that you can make the most of every moment you spend together; and how to work with difficult emotions, such as anger, jealousy and fear, so that they bring you closer together, rather than force you apart.

Most important of all, this chapter shows you how to access the emotional wisdom that is hidden within you. When you find and practise this wisdom, you will be able to turn even the most apparently hopeless situations into opportunities for transformation.

the sexual barometer

The state of a couple's sex life is often a barometer of their relationship in general. When they are happy, sexual relations between them are good, but when problems occur in other areas of their life, their sex life often suffers too. This is because sex is a form of communication, and any difficulties we have in relating emotionally to each other are magnified by the physical intimacy of sexual union. However, it is also precisely because sex is the most intimate form of physical communication that it is the ideal vehicle through which to express love for our partner.

At the start of a relationship, when your levels of sexual desire for your partner are very high, sex can be magical. But as your relationship matures and your levels of intimacy and commitment increase, the need to make love decreases and your sex life settles down. You may feel that the passion has gone, but in reality you are simply adjusting to each other's natural libidos. This is a good time to embark on a journey to explore each other's sensuality and learn how best to fulfil each other's sexual needs.

A useful way to start is to make regular dates to spend intimate time together – say, a couple of hours once or twice a week. You need to ensure that you will have total privacy, so try to arrange your dates to coincide with times when other members of the household will be out. Don't feel that you *have* to make love in these sessions – the idea is to spend time getting to rediscover each other sexually in whatever ways feel most comfortable. You might like to talk, say, about past sexual experiences or what turns you on; or you might prefer to start the date by kissing and

caressing each other tenderly and see where this touching leads you; or, again, you might wish to look at a sex manual or watch a sex video together, and talk about the positions and techniques they demonstrate. This will help you find a way to speak about your sexual desires. The more you learn about how to please each other, the more satisfying your sex life will become.

As you build up trust and physical intimacy, you can gradually introduce new elements into your love-making. Why not ask a favour of each other next time you have sex – you could ask your partner to give you a massage or to share their most erotic fantasy with you. Remember, whatever you choose to do, always approach sex with tenderness so that "making love" is a literal description of what you do together sexually.

things just as they are

Although planning for the future is an essential stage on the relationship highway, it's important not to "live" in the future (or the past), but to enjoy the experience of life as it is, in the present. When you experience the moment as it arises, you realize that the present is not just a short flash between the last moment and the next, but a spiritual dimension that opens up beyond space and time. Maybe you have encountered this in nature when the beauty of a bird's song, the majestic grandeur of a mountain, or the elemental force of waves crashing onto rocks touched you in a special way. Whenever we fully enter the present, we tune in to the very pulse of life and gain a glimpse of what Zen Buddhists term our "true nature". The ability to focus on the present moment, in a state of "mindfulness", can enrich all areas of your life, especially your love relationship.

Many of us experience intense happiness when we are first in love, because in this state we feel completely alive. It is the total awareness of the moment that enables us to feel such joy. But as our relationship matures, and life together becomes more predictable, our ability to appreciate the moment declines, and vague dissatisfaction may even creep in. By focusing our awareness on the present we can regain our lost sense of gratitude for all that is good in our relationship.

Sit down with your partner and each take a few minutes to list as many positive aspects of the relationship as you can muster. Then rank them in order of importance to you. For example, you might feel that "strong friendship" should be top of your list,

If you are unable to find the truth right where you are, where else do you expect to find it?

Dogen (1200–1253)

followed by "shared sense of humour" and "good sexual chemistry". (Don't worry if your list differs from your partner's – it's what matters to each of you individually that counts here.) Once you have completed your lists, memorize your top five positive aspects – recall them every evening before bedtime, in an act of private ritual. Train yourself not to focus on negative factors in your relationship – instead, whenever you start to feel dissatisfied, think about the good aspects. Let this evaluation be the constant background of your awareness, the "default setting" to which your mind always returns.

You can also use mindfulness to make the most of every moment together, and in so doing, learn to fully appreciate your partner. On a practical level this can mean that, instead of coming home from work and spending the evening distractedly worrying about, say, the presentation you have to give tomorrow, you give your full attention to enjoying your evening meal together and taking pleasure in each other's company. Remember, the lasting rewards of a relationship are hidden in fleeting moments of connection, which may be when your partner expresses his or her love for you through a look or a touch. If you are preoccupied, you miss these tender moments.

The art of living in the present in your relationship also means facing and embracing whatever the present contains – including any urgent issues you face. Inevitably there will be difficult periods. For example, one of you might go through a mid-life crisis during which you call into question the whole way of life on which your relationship is based. Instead of offering their support, the other partner might be tempted by this experience to deny what is happening and run away from the painful reality of the situation. Denial is a coping strategy that protects you from the full impact of suffering, but unfortunately it also keeps you frozen and unable to respond in a constructive way. This is why

there can be a strange sense of relief when you face a problem just as it is. And on the positive side, facing reality together can offer an opportunity to strengthen the relationship, no matter how dire or hopeless the circumstances first seem.

exercise 6

THE DANCE OF THE MOMENT

When you become aware of the present moment, even the most mundane tasks can become things of wonder. For example, you make a direct connection with the hot water of your shower as it tumbles onto your skin, with the sounds of the world outside your home as you walk into your own backyard, and with the smell of hot coffee as you lift the cup to your lips. This exercise teaches you and your partner how to get into the habit of being mindful by treating everything around you with tender regard.

one
When you are not spending time with your partner, but plan to meet up later, make a conscious effort to focus intently on your sensory experiences. Banish all background anxieties, and savour instead the message that all your senses are offering you – the dance of the moment.

two
When performing alone a mundane task, such as washing the dishes, making the bed, putting out the garbage, or any habitual chore that does not usually require any concentration, give the action your full attention for once. If the chore is repetitive (such as sweeping fallen leaves from the yard), concentrate on the rhythm you make.

three
Open yourself to what you are doing, no matter how ordinary. Enjoy the rightness of the action – the fact that you are doing something necessary, constructive, time-honoured. Listen to the sounds generated by the chore, and be aware of the movements of your own muscles as you work. If you find your mind wandering, gently bring it back to focus on the job in hand.

four
When you at last see your partner again, allow your spell of mindfulness to flood over into your experience of meeting each other. Focus on nothing but the kiss or hug with which you greet each other. You will probably find that you are intensely aware of this sudden reunion with the person you love. Savour the wonderful moments of this reunion.

the corrective lens of values

Our values form the moral code by which we live our lives. They are instilled in us when we are children by our parents or guardians, teachers and other people of influence and authority. When you act in accordance with your values, you experience a sense of stability and rightness; when you go against them, you feel uneasy and guilty. This is straightforward enough. The problems start when you enter a relationship and find that some of your values clash with those of your partner. For example, your partner might think it clever to outsmart business associates using tactics you consider unethical, whereas he or she might feel that your honest, altogether kinder approach is far too soft and indulgent. Discovering where your values differ from your partner's and finding an acceptable compromise is an integral part of being realistic about your relationship.

Making conscious choices about values is a mark of an evolving human being. But to do so in the context of a relationship, you need to explore both your own and your partner's values. To help you pinpoint your moral codes, each note the first answers that spring to mind in response to the following statements:

- "It is important to be ... " (list at least ten qualities here)
- "Sometimes it's OK to be ... " (list at least three adjectives)
- "A home should always be ... " (list at least three adjectives)
- "Beware of ... people, as they are usually ... " (this will reveal your hidden prejudices)
- "My parents used to say that we should always be ..." (list at least three items).

Now assess your instinctive responses to see if they still ring true, by giving them a score from 1 to 5, 1 meaning "I disagree completely" and 5 meaning "I agree completely." Then rate each other's statements from 1 to 5. Next take three different-coloured pens and use the first to list the values that, according to your answers, you hold in common. Then, in the second colour, add the values that you partly agree on. Finally, in the third colour, list those values that one holds while the other doesn't – these are the potential problem areas in your relationship. Reflect together on moments when your different values caused discord and discuss how you could each modify your position to move closer together and live more harmoniously.

springing the gender trap

Gender is one of the cultural filters through which we see life. An understanding of what it is to be a man or a woman is central to understanding ourselves and others. It is also essential to the formation of a good relationship.

Gender stereotypes are passed on in subtle ways through the behaviour of our parents and through society as a whole. Despite the suffragette movement in the early twentieth century and the women's liberation movement which started in the 1960s, many little girls in the West are still taught that they must be gentle and sensitive to others, not bossy or boastful. And many little boys are still encouraged not to cry or show emotion, but to be assertive, even aggressive. Although we may consciously reject such stereotyping as we grow up, it is often deeply embedded in the psyche. It is hardly surprising, then, that gender issues can be a source of conflict with your partner.

In a love relationship there is a fundamental need to be loved and accepted. Both men and women fear that if they behave in a way that is perceived as unattractive by their partner, they will be rejected. And such fears trap people in roles "expected" of their gender. To comply with such stereotypes, we may be forced to go against our better instincts and adapt our actions and demeanour to fit a profile we find uncomfortable. This can make us feel both frustrated and angry – emotions that cause discord and provoke arguments with our partner. It is always beneficial, therefore, to try to remain true to ourselves, both for our own wellbeing and for the good of the relationship.

You can start by reassessing whether you are adopting certain roles out of gender habit or because they are how you really wish to be. The woman's roles in housework and childcare are obvious key issues where gender expectations are brought into focus. Many couples might feel that they are in the vanguard of gender equality, the man doing many of the household chores, the woman earning a good wage, and both giving enlightened time to any children they might have. In fact, the old straightjackets are not necessarily discarded, sometimes merely loosened.

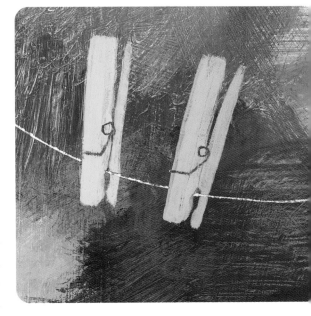

To analyze the degree to which gender is a determining factor in your relationship, ask yourself some searching questions. Yes, the man might contribute to the running of the house, but does he perform anything like half the labour? Who does the cleaning? Who notices what parts of the home need cleaning? (These last two questions are very different from each other.) Who does the cooking? Who runs the storecupboard? Who pays the bills? Who worries about whether the bills are accurate and reasonable? (Again, related issues, but with significant differences.) The underlying point in the last six examples is that even where labour is distributed fairly, the responsible thinking behind the labour may fall to one partner or another along gender lines.

Despite the survival of gender-stereotyping in many areas of life, it is true that in the West we are moving toward a more open

society where roles are less clearly prescribed by convention. More and more men are finding happiness nurturing their families, and more and more women are winning respect for themselves in traditionally male-dominated professions.

In parallel with these developments, gender-based mindsets are fraying at the edges in an interesting fashion. Men now have social sanction to display their emotions, even their weaknesses; while women are allowed to be tough, pragmatic, down-to-earth. It is worth asking yourselves how, if at all, your relationship has been deepened by such freedoms and, conversely, what benefit or pleasure you each derive from traditional gender expectations (see exercise, opposite). Accelerating social changes over the last century have made male-female relationships potentially more flexible and homosexual relationships potentially less stigmatized. If you feel, nevertheless, that social pressures are preventing you from being fully yourself within the context of your relationship, ask your partner if he or she feels the same and try to discuss the matter openly.

Biology, of course, can never be liberalized (although attitudes to biology can). Living in a male or female body radically affects our perception of the world. One area in which experiences are very different according to whether you are male or female, is sex. If your partner is of the other gender, make a point of discovering as much as you can about sex from his or her perspective. Try to discuss the matter openly and honestly. The more you are able to bridge the gender gap, the closer you will become.

exercise 7

CONFRONTING YOUR STEREOTYPES

Although we might think that we have broken free of gender-stereotyping, it is only when we pinpoint our ideas and expectations about male and female behaviour that our true views become apparent. This exercise will help you and your partner to examine your deep-seated attitudes to gender and to explore your potential outside the limitations of gender-stereotyping. You will need some paper and two pens.

one
Each take a piece of paper and a pen. Now complete the following statements,
listing three facets of behaviour for each:
Men normally ...
Women normally ...
Men don't normally ...
Women don't normally ...
I like men who ...
I like women who ...
I dislike men who ...
I dislike women who ...
Ideally, men should ...
Ideally, women should ...

two
Now go through these statements carefully with your partner and discuss what you have
each put and why. How similar are your responses? Do you broadly agree or disagree in
your attitudes? What did you learn about yourself? Do either of you feel that the
exercise has revealed any surprising prejudices?

three
Analyze any ways in which your views might have caused discord within your relationship.
How can you modify your expectations so that you can live more harmoniously together?
Encourage each other to develop in ways that open up more options within the
relationship, disregarding gender stereotypes.

expanding your world of interest

In the rush of modern life we may feel that we have to push our-selves just to keep up with our commitments and responsibilities, and the thought of taking up a new interest might seem daunt-ing. But bear in mind that your relationship, if locked into the routine of everyday life, will have less room to grow or develop. By expanding your personal horizons, you set yourselves inter-esting places to which you can travel together.

One of the most rewarding ways to share time with someone is to move forward in step – to explore new ideas or activities, to build on mutual enthusiasms, to exchange ideas in response to new stimuli. The more time you spend with each other, the more opportunities you will have to feed on developing interests in a mutual dialogue – a commentary of shared experience.

Why not learn a new skill together? Or perhaps a way to combine two different concerns and explore their complemen-tarity. For example, if one of you is interested in Spanish and the other in history, you might start to get involved in the discover-ies of Christopher Columbus – perhaps prompted by a TV pro-gram or an exhibition.

Try to shape a menu of joint interests with equal emphasis on the physical and the intellectual, the fun and the creative, the social and the solitary. Create some deliberately cross-grain effects in your life – that is to say, take something that lies at the very edge of your personality (perhaps an incipient interest in swing bands, butterflies or rollerblading) and try moving this from background to foreground. Develop it as a new interest, and

The greatest joy is not only to love each other, but together to love the world.

Anonymous

relish the incongruity – the way it stands out as exceptional against the pattern of your other preoccupations. Relish, too, the unusual lines of communication it opens up with your partner.

A couple with a well-rounded assortment of interests has a better chance of staying together. Some of your shared interests will be predominantly yours, while in others it will be your partner who takes the lead. Even when you go off alone in your own direction, try to be wholehearted. After immersing yourself in an activity you enjoy, your sense of achievement and ensuing good mood will have a positive effect on your partner, too.

personality – the recognizable you

By definition, personality is one of our constant features – we might change our appearance, our weight, even our gender, but our personality traits accompany us faithfully throughout life. So runs the received wisdom on the subject.

It follows that people in a healthy relationship accept each other's personalities as they are. If, say, your partner is a party animal, you know that there is little point in persuading him or her to spend a two-week vacation alone with you in the mountains, communing with nature. The realistic way to have a harmonious life together is to try to understand and appreciate your partner's personality (as well as your own), and to change your lifestyle to accommodate any significant differences of personality between you.

A useful tool for looking at personality in connection with relationships is the Myers Briggs Type Indicator (MBTI), which was developed in the 1940s by Katherine Briggs and Isabel Briggs Myers, based on the work of the Swiss psychologist Carl Jung (1875–1961). The MBTI describes four pairs of personality traits. To assess yourselves on the scale, take time together and, each of you individually, address the questions below. The answers will show you and your partner your own personality profiles. Once you have reached these conclusions, you can begin to understand the dynamics of your relationship in a new way.

Here are the questions. First, would you say that you are **an Extrovert or an Introvert?** Where is your energy naturally directed – inward or outward? Extroverts direct their energy

primarily toward things and people outside themselves. They like to be around people and are easily distracted. Conversely, Introverts direct their energy largely inward, toward their own feelings and thoughts. They are comfortable spending time alone and are able to concentrate well.

Next, are you **a Sensor or an Intuitive?** Sensors have good common sense and tend to be practical and realistic. Intuitives, on the other hand, trust their instinct and are creative and ideal-istic. Now consider how you make decisions. Are you **a Thinker or a Feeler?** Thinkers tend to be analytical, logical, objective and driven by achievement. Feelers are warm, sensitive, empathetic, and motivated by being appreciated. And finally, what approach to experience do you take? Are you **a Judger or a Perceiver?** Judgers tend to be productive and organized, whereas Perceivers tend to be flexible, playful and *dis*organized.

When you have each measured yourselves against the four personality benchmarks, compare notes. There is usually little friction in a relationship if your personalities are similar – in fact, your relationship could end up being rather dull. However, friction means heat and fire: that is, both disagreement and passion. So while you may be in for a challenging ride if your personality types differ, you will also have a potentially passionate and

 compelling relationship. For example, you may be a Judger, who likes to plan, while your partner prefers to be spontaneous and, say, whisk you away for romantic weekends at a moment's notice.

You could, of course, spend a whole lifetime moaning that your partner isn't more like you! But if you do so, you are missing the point – you unconsciously chose your partner as a teacher or counterweight so that you could develop your missing personality traits and become whole.

As you take a look at your profiles together, ask your partner which aspects of your personality they find most difficult to live with. This will highlight some of the negative aspects of your personality, such as laziness, carelessness, thoughtlessness and so on, which, with a little effort, you *can* learn to change. It may be hard to accept what your partner says, but remind yourself that he or she is offering you a useful insight. When your partner points out one of your personality traits that they find problematic, try to find a practical solution that suits you both. If, say, you know that you have a tendency to recklessness – you act first and think later – it might be unrealistic to try to transform yourself into someone who carefully assesses every situation before taking action. But you *could* probably learn to take a slightly more measured approach. This would be of benefit to you both because you would gain a degree of control over your reckless streak and your partner would gain confidence in your ability to act in a more considered way.

Learning to understand and take into account your partner's personality traits will help you to overcome obstacles together and reinforce the bonds of your relationship.

THE FOUNDATIONS OF LOVE

According to psychologist John Bowlby, our first experiences of forming attachments strongly influence both our personalities and our behaviour in adult relationships. "Secure" babies enjoy contact with their parents, confident that these adults will offer refuge in frightening situations. Such children grow up into adults who find it easy to get close to others. But, if their initial bonding is characterized by uncertainty, babies form "anxious" attachments: they feel unsure whether their parents will be there when they need them. As adults such people tend to cling to their partners. Babies who have come to expect that their parents will not be there for them form "avoidant" attachments, showing little reaction to being separated from any particular person. "Avoidant" adults find it difficult to form close relationships.

responsibility – a joint effort

There is a tendency in all of us to blame others when things go wrong. And because our partner is closest to us, he or she often bears the brunt of such blame. But the fact of the matter is that we are each responsible for our own actions; and within a relationship both partners are equally responsible for the success of that enterprise. When life does not work out as we had planned, it is more constructive to regard your partner as an ally than as an obstacle or an irrelevance. After all, as two boats that have chosen to negotiate the same ocean currents together, there is much to be gained from your implied promise of mutual support.

Often the problem we face, even when it has no direct bearing on the relationship itself, exerts a strain upon our partnership. Difficulties at work provide a good example of the kinds of situation that might develop. Imagine that a new recruit to your company is being favoured over you, has been placed on the fast track to advancement, and is likely to be given the senior position on which you have set your sights. How does this impact upon your relationship? Well, for one thing, it is likely to make you preoccupied, even irritable – and you might find it harder to respond to your partner's enthusiasms. Then again, you might be annoyed when your partner, in an attempt to console or reassure, gets the situation slightly out of perspective, through not knowing the full facts. At a deeper level, your self-esteem might be impaired – perhaps you feel that you are disappointing your partner by failing to move smoothly up the career ladder. Finally, of course, there is the question of money, which brings the

practical effect of losing the sought-after senior position firmly into the shared realm.

Now, in such a situation, the first thing to do is describe your predicament to your loved one, and benefit from the empathy you are likely to receive. Do not simply express anger at your boss – this will leave your partner feeling excluded, because they will be unable to share in it. Instead, show your emotional need, as something to which they can perfectly respond. Accept with gratitude the gestures that are offered – think of them as blessings. Then, having received the well-directed impulses of healing, try to regain a balanced perspective. The life you share with your partner, after all, is not the life you share with your work

For one human being to love another – that is perhaps the most difficult of our tasks; the ultimate, the last test of proof; the work for which all other work is but preparation.

Rainer Maria Rilke (1875–1926)

colleagues. You are now in a realm in which promotion or otherwise has no real presence, only a reflected presence. You are in a world in which you can be unreservedly happy.

If, conversely, you are in the position of giving rather than seeking support, follow this basic sequence. First, your alertness will tell you that something is amiss. Gently ask what it is and whether you can help. Listen (see pp.102–3 on the skill of "deep listening") – to both what is said and what isn't said. Put yourself empathetically in his or her shoes. Make gestures, physical and verbal, to reiterate your love and show your support. Take your cue from everything that you hear and observe. Make allowances. Hasten to show that he or she has lost no credit in your eyes.

As well as empathizing, your responsibilities toward your partner may include offering constructive advice, but *only* if so requested (it can be irritating to be told what to do when you prefer to find your own solution). If problem-solving input *is* invited, brainstorm together to come up with as many options as possible. However, ultimately it is up to your partner to decide how to proceed, and you must respect that decision.

Even the most solid relationships can be rocked by stressful events that hit you out of the blue – everything from bereavement and serious illness to the discovery that your child is on drugs. The first thing to do is remind yourselves that you have a strong bond and that you can come through this together. Next, talk about the problem openly and honestly – let all your feelings out and acknowledge them. Once you have gone through this cathartic process, you will be more able to make an action

plan. If you both feel at a loss about how to proceed, seek help from a relevant agency – professional advice can help you tackle the problem together in the most effective way.

During such periods of crisis, try to avoid being completely swamped by the problem. Bear in mind that anxiety in itself can never resolve any difficulties – it can only reflect uncertainty, about either what to do or what the future holds. If you are uncertain what to do, work through the possibilities, make a decision, and put your anxieties behind you. Making a positive choice should also allay any worries you might have about the future, as your commitment to the relationship gives you a strong bulwark against the storms of fortune.

the changing weather of emotions

Love, joy, excitement, hurt, fear and boredom are just some of the emotions that most people experience in their relationship at some point or other. Take five minutes now to list all the emotions that you remember having had over the past week. If you are honest with yourself, you will probably be surprised at the length and variety of your list.

Above all, clothe yourselves with love, which binds everything together in perfect harmony.

Colossians 3:14

The ever-changing weather of emotions can be one of the most difficult aspects of a relationship. You are out together, enjoying a pleasant time, laughing and exchanging harmless remarks. But then one thoughtless, inconsequential remark acts as a trigger, and a squall of emotion is released from one of you, coming out of nowhere. The atmosphere of your togetherness changes dramatically. It is hard to pitch harmless words across the sudden divide: they either make things worse, or they fall uselessly into the void, unheeded.

While you can't realistically expect your partner to be constant in his or her feelings and reactions, you *can* learn to deal with emotional peaks and troughs successfully. Furthermore, by working together to develop emotional wisdom in your relationship, you can turn negative feelings into positive ones.

Emotional wisdom means gaining insight into your own emotions. It is a matter of learning to manage your moods and of using the information that your emotions offer you as signposts to change. (While an emotion is a strong, but often fleeting feeling, a mood is a feeling that has settled in and become a state of mind.) Emotional wisdom helps you find a positive way to deal with your emotions without resorting to repression or self-indulgence; and also gives you the skills to recognize and handle effectively the emotions of your partner and others.

A good starting point for gaining emotional wisdom is to discover your habitual emotional patterns. You can do this by keeping a mood journal. Take the six basic emotions (fear, anger, happiness, disgust, surprise, sadness) as well as love, and for a period of at least a week, keep a daily record of how often you experience each of them: 1 being the score for never, 2 rarely, 3 sometimes, 4 often, 5 constantly. This will give you an insight into your basic emotional pattern. It is useful to write your mood journals together, because your partner will often have a

clearer perspective of your emotional states than you yourself have. Once you have both completed your process of monitoring in this way, discuss and analyze the results together. Now decide whether the emotional patterns that have emerged are ones that you would choose voluntarily. If not, resolve to become more aware of your feelings as they are happening, so that you can begin to gain much more control over them.

A key skill of emotional wisdom is good communication. The ability to express our feelings is integral to a successful relationship. Most of us are adept at sharing our positive emotions – such as happiness on, say, learning that we have won an important contract at work, or joy because, say, our sister has had a baby. But we have trouble sharing our negative emotions. When you realize that you are in a difficult mood, one of the most effective ways to avoid causing discord is to be honest. For example, say to your partner: "I'm feeling very irritable today, and I don't really know why." By doing this, you have acknowledged the problem and have begun to stand back and take an overview. And by involving your partner, you are suddenly on the same side, both of you noting, observing and trying to understand your emotional inner landscape.

If it is difficult to understand your own emotions, it can be even more so to fathom your partner's. When your partner is being difficult for no apparent reason, step back from your own angry or defensive response for a moment and try to empathize with him or her. No matter how irrational or unprovoked their emotional outburst might seem to you, it is totally justified and very real to them – so try to imagine yourself in their situation. Does the outburst begin to make more sense? Drawing on your knowledge of your partner's character, proceed in the way that is least likely to add fuel to the fire. For example, if they seem to be expecting an apology from you for something you have allegedly said or done, say that you are sorry, even if you feel that an apology is unjustified. Then leave your partner to calm down –

you can return to the matter later. If you interpret your partner's emotional behaviour as a need for reassurance, gently offer comfort. If this is what they seem to want, allow them to talk about their feelings and whatever caused them; otherwise, let them know that you are there if they need you and allow them some space. Knowing when you can help by discussing something together and when to leave your partner to work things through on their own is another important aspect of emotional wisdom.

If you are tempted to persevere with a discussion when all your partner's signals say, "Leave me alone, I don't want to talk about this any more," desist! Any attempt at probing would be pointless and could make matters worse. The pragmatic solution in such circumstances is to back off and let your partner sort out their emotions in their own time and manner – just look out for the sign that they are ready to start sharing again.

THE MIRROR TEST

Try standing in front of a mirror – a full-length one, if possible – and replay a recent disagreement with your partner, or invent an imaginary scenario if you prefer. Relive the conversation in as much detail as possible and allow your face and body to move naturally in the way that they did, or would have done, at each stage of this exchange. Study your reflection and note any expressions or poses that you find surprising – try to see yourself through the eyes of your partner and imagine how you would react to the person you see in the mirror. Encourage your partner to work through the mirror exercise as well, ideally using the same situation as a stimulus. Then share your reactions.

reading body language

Emotions, and the ways in which we show them, are complex. Recent research has found that while the facial expressions of the six basic emotions – fear, anger, happiness, disgust, surprise, sadness – are recognized instantly by almost all human beings, there are more than thirty further facial expressions that we might use. We also display our emotions in our posture – the way we sit, or the positions of our arms, legs and head. Sometimes the message signalled by our posture or expression can be at odds with that suggested by our tone of voice or the actual words we are saying. This is because we often try to regulate or hide our real emotions. Is it any wonder, then, that reading each other's feelings correctly can seem such a complicated undertaking?

Sometimes you may find that your partner reacts to you in a way you find perplexing. What might seem to you a calm discussion can slide swiftly into tension. It may be that some aspect of your body language of which you are unaware has started this opposition. A frown, however fleeting, might be perceived as an expression of hostility or reluctance; a shrug of the shoulders might be taken to mean that you don't care. By understanding better how other people are likely to interpret your facial expressions and bodily postures, you have a better chance of avoiding misunderstandings in the future.

Avoid the trap of trying to limit your body language because you feel it gives away too many of your secrets – this is merely a recipe for becoming less expressive. Use your hands freely, as

Mediterranean people often do – the hands are eloquent, with a language of their own. Try also to encourage the mobility of your face. Usually, these approaches have more to do with loosening a habitual rigidity than with acquiring an entirely new means of communication. Body language already lies latent within you – it is a matter not of putting on an unfamiliar act but of shedding unnecessary inhibitions. You will find, as you use your hands and face more in support of spoken language, that you are more accurately expressing and more deeply feeling whatever it is you have to convey.

controlling your anger

The key to handling anger in a relationship is to learn how to deal with the intensity of your feelings in a way that minimizes their effect on your partner. Let's take a look at how to do this. When an argument breaks out between you, and you feel overwhelmed with anger, a good way to deal with the situation is just to walk away. Halt the confrontation by taking a few deep breaths and calmly informing your partner, "I'm feeling very angry right now and I need to have a short break." Then, simply go to another room or out for a walk. Or if you are stuck in a car, state clearly that you wish to be silent for a while. It is important that your partner doesn't feel that you are turning your back on the relationship or punishing them in some way, because this would simply fuel their resentment. Make it clear that you will return and resume the discussion once you have had some time out in which to calm down and think the matter through.

During this solitary interlude you might find it useful to perform a breathing exercise or visualization to help you regain your composure. Concentrating fully on the act of breathing, take at least five slow, deep breaths, then turn your awareness inward and monitor what is going on. Notice the thoughts whirling around in your mind and the anger seething in the pit of your stomach. Placing your hand on your stomach, acknowledge and accept your anger, then try to let it disperse. It might be helpful if you visualize your feelings disappearing in some way – for example, floating away in bubbles. After a while, the rage will subside.

Now ask yourself, "What other emotions fuelled this anger? What was the trigger?" You will probably find that hurt, fear, shame or some other emotion lies at the root of your anger. Identify and acknowledge this hidden feeling and gently explore where it came from. The more you can accept whatever feelings lay at the root of your anger, the easier it will be to talk about them with your partner.

When the heat has died down, return to your partner and discuss your findings. Admit that you lost your temper, apologize for anything hurtful you said or did, and try to explain the underlying emotions that provoked your anger. Be truthful about your partner's precise role in these emotions. Ask about his or her feelings too. Finally, look at how you could both manage a similar situation more effectively next time.

THE ANGER WORK–OUT

The body reacts to anger in much the same way as to fear – by releasing the hormone epinephrine (adrenaline) into the bloodstream. And like fear, anger often causes a build-up of aggressive feelings. But this primeval response is no longer appropriate in the 21st century. Most cultures today frown on the physical expression of anger through violence. One of the most effective ways in which to release this emotion is through exercise. If you are finding it difficult to manage your anger, why not try a sport? By taking up karate, or learning to hit a tennis ball hard and fast across court, you can vent your feelings, acquire a new skill and improve your fitness, all at the same time.

taming your jealousy

Jealousy is the fear we feel when we perceive that someone else has, has had or might one day have – jealousy does not confine itself to a simple present tense – the affection of our partner. In other words, it is related to loss. In the event of physical disloyalty, whether real or imagined, there is also a sense of outrage. To experience jealousy is to suffer. In its extreme form, it is like being locked in a furnace, consumed by flames of rage, anxiety and suspicion. We have been usurped; our self-image plummets. If we do not know all the facts, we are pulled in two opposite directions – desire, on the one hand, to have our worst suspicions confirmed; on the other, to have them proved wrong. How then can we tame this complex, self-destructive emotion which gnaws away at the very fabric of our relationship?

The first thing is to remind yourself that, unless you have proof of unfaithfulness, your jealousy is based on a *perception*, not on a reality. If you are jealous by nature, you might be reading into your partner's actions a significance that doesn't exist. For example, let us say that recently he or she has started going to the gym more often, and that this keenness has coincided with an attractive instructor starting work there. You have seen them laughing together after class on a couple of occasions. You might start to imagine the worst. But, when you consider the bare facts, you have to accept that your partner is only being friendly.

In arriving at this conclusion, you might realize that it is, in fact, your jealousy that is the problem. If so, you will make little progress by telling your partner how you feel and asking them

for practical reassurance (by spending less time at the gym or by changing classes). Better to live by the trust you claim to invest in your relationship. If you know that you are suffering from an emotional affliction, why visit this upon your partner? Instead, try and acclimatize yourself to their friendships – perhaps by encouraging situations where you can all socialize together. In the meantime, work on your self-esteem: unfounded jealousy almost always stems from a profound insecurity, a sense of being unworthy. The most effective way to sustain a healthy relationship is by discovering who it is exactly your partner is in love with – in other words, by getting to know and be yourself more fully than ever before.

Nobody can love who is not jealous.

André le Chapelain
(13th century)

overcoming your fears

 At some stage in your relationship, fear in one form or another is likely to surface and undermine your happiness. Let's have a look at the most common types of fear that occur in relationships and consider some possible ways in which to overcome them.

By far the most prevalent relationship fear is the fear of being rejected by or losing your partner. When it first dawns upon you that you are deeply in love with a person and find them totally irresistible, it is difficult not to assume that everyone else must feel the same way about them too. And so you fear that someone "better" will entice them away from you. Or, when you are about to make a commitment – say, when you are on the verge of deciding to live together – you fear that cementing the relationship in this way will somehow make your partner feel tied down and scare them off. Or, when your relationship has stood the test of time and you feel happy and settled, you might one day suddenly be afraid that your loved one could fall ill and die.

Take a moment now to reflect on your relationship fears, and write down the five worst. Now, taking each of these in turn, ask yourself these questions: what would I do if this happened? How would I cope? Who would help? Who would I talk to? Who would be sympathetic? How would life be a month later? A year later? Through these questions you are facing up to your worst fears; and by making contingency plans in case any of these fears is actually realized, you are taking away much of their power over you.

Another common relationship problem (almost the opposite of fear of loss)
is fear of commitment. This can arise
from a bad experience in a previous
relationship, whether as a child with a
domineering parent, or as an adult with
a previous, overly possessive partner. It
may also stem from low self-esteem –
you believe that you don't deserve to be
loved. The way to deal with this type of
commitment fear is to probe through
your past, try to pinpoint the cause and,

again, face the fear. This can take courage, but it is well worth it,
because once you can accept whatever happened in your past
and move on, you will be free to be truly present in your relationship. There is a third cause of commitment fear – that, deep
down, you think you might have made the wrong choice of partner. If this is truly the case, you owe it both to yourself and to
your partner to be honest, to admit your doubts and to walk
away from the relationship.

A further type of fear that requires consideration is the fear of
violence (not just physical abuse, but also verbal, as well as threat-
ening behaviour and shouting). If you feel that your partner has
a problem with violence, take a firm stand. Demand that they
take a course in anger management or undergo counselling to
learn to control themselves. If they do not agree to seek help, it
might be best to leave the relationship until they do. Love cannot survive in an atmosphere of fear.

a home that works

A home is much more than just a group of furnished rooms in which you live: it is a sanctuary where you can feel safe and relaxed enough to be yourself. When you share your living space with your partner, it is important that you both feel completely comfortable with the way you run your home. This way, it becomes a place where the relationship can grow and flourish.

After you have been together for a while, it is tempting to accept the way that your home works (in particular, how you divide chores) without questioning whether you are doing things in the way that is best for your relationship. This can lead to a pattern of recurrent niggles, which in turn creates friction between you. It is a therefore a good idea to take time together to review the way you run your home.

First, see what improvements you can realistically make to promote more quality time together. For example, perhaps simply by re-scheduling say, the weekly shopping trip to the superstore from a Saturday morning to an evening after work, you can manage to spend the whole of Saturday together. You could also give each other a fresh perspective on the relationship by swapping roles in some of your household duties. Perhaps, if you habitually cook the evening meal, your partner could take on this responsibility for a week and you could instead wash the dishes, a job your partner usually does. By exchanging tasks in this way, you will each gain an insight into any frustrations suffered by the other and learn to value what he or she does, so that you take each other less for granted.

You also need to make sure that the chores are divided fairly. The best way to ensure that you both pull your weight domestically is to draw up a list of all the weekly household tasks, noting beside each one the approximate time it takes. Then examine the current division of labour, and if either of you is unhappy with it, try to divide up the tasks more equally. Or if you prefer, you could devise two separate rotas of tasks which you alternate, week by week. Or you could write all the chores on cards, and draw your quota randomly at the beginning of each week. Above all, try to share chores in a new spirit of light-heartedness and goodwill.

Spending time and money on home décor is something happy couples tend to do more than unhappy couples. A joint project of this kind, often requiring compromise in matters of taste, will only run smoothly if the couple are in tune with each other emotionally. Remember, too, that a "gift" made by one partner to the home – a new labour-saving appliance or a display of flowers – is a gift to the other person too, as well as a celebration of the harmonious lifestyle you share. Surprises like this are low-risk compared with, for example, a complete room make-over – only make such grand gestures if you are absolutely sure of your loved one's taste. Performing a task can also be a gift – especially when it is something that could have been left indefinitely, but whose completion contributes to the home's appeal.

how to rethink what you want

The gap between what we think we want and how our life really is can breed heartache and discontent. The pursuit of fantasies can lead to unhappiness, whereas joy and peacefulness greet us when we accept the gift of the moment, even when it presents a challenge. Being realistic requires you to dispel far-fetched expectations – the belief that happiness makes every moment glow with energy, that your partner is capable of becoming the idealized figure you were looking for when you were single, that sharing love gives you an invisible magic mantle that absolves you from having to develop yourself or work at your relationship to keep it healthy. Positive realism entails putting great effort into your relationship, so that even in the midst of difficulty you never lose sight of the potential for happiness, and indeed regularly *feel* happy – in the knowledge that what you share with your partner has value beyond measure.

At the heart of this awakening to happiness is the process of rethinking what we think we want. Wishes that have no chance of being realized are burdens to us, weighing us down in proportion to the amount of time we spend daydreaming in their treacherous half-light. While wrapping our thoughts around such pointless dreams, we risk neglecting the genuine opportunities.

So how can we learn to enjoy, appreciate and improve on what we already have in our relationship? How can we distinguish false dreams from positive and realistic aspirations? The following process will help you and your partner clarify the difference. Each ask yourself, "What do I really need to be happy

in my relationship?" and compile a list – without distinguishing the things you already have from the things that you are seeking. This list will most probably consist mainly of relationship qualities, such as passion, respect, intimacy and so on; but it can also include aspects of fulfilment, such as a good job; and practical considerations, such as someone to babysit one evening a week.

Now adopt a more ruthless and realistic attitude. Each of you must take each item in turn and ask yourself whether or not you think you could experience happiness without it. Cross out anything on the list to which you can reply "yes". You will find that your lists becomes shorter and shorter. And as you let go of most of the conditions you had set for happiness, your chances of reaching the goal increase dramatically. When you have both

finished reducing your lists in this way, take each entry and consider in what circumstances you could be happy without it. This will make you realize that most of the things you feel you need to achieve happiness in the relationship would actually be unnecessary if only certain other things could be better. When you are left with the lists of items that you feel are really fundamental to your happiness, share them with your partner. Some of these things you will have already: cross them off the list in a spirit of mutual thanksgiving. The remaining items left on the list constitute your constructive wishes for change. If there are any items that you both have on your lists, brainstorm together on how you could create these qualities or conditions in your relationship – they should be the easiest to bring to fruition because both of you share such a strong desire for them. Tackle these items first.

The final stage of the exercise is for each of you to put the remaining items – the ones that are your individual rather than shared requirements – in order of priority. These are your personal blueprints for happiness. It is right that your partner should know about them, and help you put them into effect. You now have a common plan and two personal plans. The common plan is where two sets of wishes coincide – what could be more powerful as a program of mutual fulfilment? You have now only to start putting your shared program into action – in a spirit of positive and harmonious cooperation.

exercise 8

STREAMLINING YOUR GOALS

The process of reassessing what we really want in our relationship involves taking stock of our hopes and expectations and letting go of anything that we feel is no longer necessary for our happiness or that is patently unrealistic. Try the following visualization to help you let go of even long-cherished desires that no longer form part of your vision for the future of your relationship.

one

Find a quiet place where you can lie down or sit comfortably. You might like to play some soothing music in the background to set the mood. Now centre yourself by focusing on your breathing for 2 minutes. Be attentive to how you take in each breath and then, as you exhale, how you let it go.

two

Next, think about the hopes or desires that you wish to release, and imagine that you are holding a number of coloured balloons, each of which represents one of these redundant attachments.

three

Release the balloons, one by one, into the air. Watch them gently float upward and disappear into the sky. Be aware of your emotions: are you relieved? Do you feel as if a weight has been lifted from your shoulders? Or is there a tinge of regret for what might have been? No matter how you react, acknowledge these feelings honestly.

four

Now spend 2 minutes thinking about your positive plans for your future together and how you intend to turn your constructive wish for change into a reality.

relationship strategies

Strategy is the ally, not the enemy, of love. When you follow a strategy, you put constructive energy into achieving your most heartfelt wishes. The term, in another context, might suggest cold calculation, even deceit. Here it is totally innocent of such connotations. A relationship strategy is simply a practical principle designed to facilitate the success of the relationship, to the benefit of both parties.

In this chapter you learn ten strategies that will enable you to transform your lives together, and also give you new insight into how to develop your individual potential. Each strategy includes a practical exercise. The strategies are designed to help you establish positive relationship habits that will encourage love to grow and flourish. They will make you feel closer to each other. They will enrich the time you spend together and the time you spend apart. And they will help you to avoid common pitfalls that any couple might otherwise fall into.

how to use the strategies

Strategies are carefully thought-out approaches that help you achieve your goals. The following repertoire of ten relationship strategies amounts to a program for building a secure, rewarding, loving union with your partner, without neglecting to develop your own unique potential. If you are planning to work with your partner through this chapter, establish a regular time each week when you can read the strategies and follow the exercises together. I suggest you start with Strategy 1 (Closeness), then move on to Strategy 2 (Appreciation), as these are fundamental to relationship harmony and cannot be overlooked. After that, either continue working through the strategies in sequence or pick out the ones that seem most relevant to your circumstances.

Each strategy highlights one aspect of a relationship and shows how to improve it. For example, if you are having difficulty communicating with each other, work through strategies 4 (Honesty) and 5 (Dialogue). These two approaches show you, among other things, how to listen attentively to your partner without becoming defensive and how to speak the truth without apportioning blame. Or, if your main concern is to improve the quality of the time you spend together and prevent various outside pressures from blighting your relationship, try strategies 7 (Time) and 9 (Play). If your relationship has lost its sparkle, add some spice to your love by following Strategy 10 (Surprise), which can help you to rediscover your sense of fun.

Sometimes one partner is more willing to put energy into the relationship than the other. However, even though a relationship

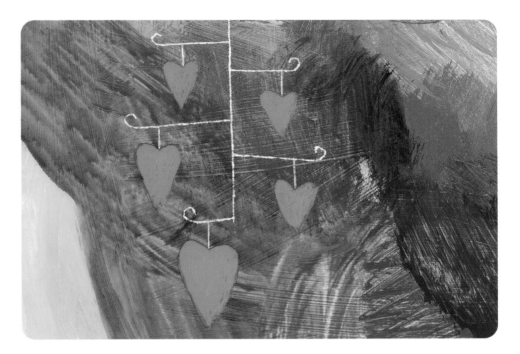

will grow faster if both partners are equally keen to change, there can still be a significant improvement if only one partner puts in the special effort. A relationship is like a mobile – if you move just one part, this has a knock-on effect, and all the parts start to swing and settle in a new place. In the same way, if you yourself change, the person who plays such a key part in your life will also change in response.

Whatever your situation, your age, and whether or not you live together or have children at home, the strategies will change how you relate to yourself, as well as to your partner, and teach you to love in a new way based on harmony, understanding and truth. Good relationships evolve naturally, but can always be further strengthened; flawed relationships can always be repaired.

strategy 1: closeness

*Love is the bridge
between two hearts.*

Anonymous

Closeness is more than physical proximity: it is the feeling that you can be wholly yourself in your partner's company, that just being together has natural positive value. If you lack this feeling, you can be like strangers going through the motions of sharing a life without the warmth of intimacy. Closeness takes many forms: physical, emotional, intellectual, social and spiritual. Each of these types is potent and can enrich a relationship in a different way. Ideally, you should aim to develop closeness in all these areas, but in practice most couples tend to be close in some ways and not in others. Focus on your weakest forms of closeness first. Bear in mind that for most couples the most important types of closeness to cultivate are emotional and physical.

There is no doubt that human beings feel closest to each other when they enjoy body contact. As babies we are happiest when we are cuddled up, skin to skin, with our mother or father. And throughout adult life we continue to derive a sense of security and comfort from physical closeness with others. Unfortunately, most couples touch each other less and less as their relationship matures, and their emotional remoteness tends to increase with this loss of physical contact.

To help rediscover physical and emotional closeness, why not start a new routine of hugging each other? You can start by hugging whenever one of you leaves the home or returns. Try to stay in the hug for at least two full inbreaths and outbreaths. Allow yourself to relax and focus all your attention on the sensations of warmth and closeness. If you are physically stronger or bigger

than your partner, make sure that you do not overwhelm or constrict them. Once you have developed the habit of hugging each other at certain times, you will find that you start to touch each other more often, in a more spontaneous way.

Now stop and ask yourself how often you kiss your partner. I don't mean a routine peck on the cheek, I mean a real, tender, magical kiss on the lips! Have you ever asked your partner how they like to be kissed? If not, make a point of finding out now. It is a well-known fact that many women are unhappy with the way their partner kisses them but never say so directly! Kissing is a wonderful way to foster closeness, especially if you do it in a sensitive way. Keep your lips soft and supple and let your approach be gentle and caring so that your partner can reciprocate with tenderness. Use your tongue only when you wish to signal that you would prefer a more sexual encounter.

Of course, satisfying sex is a great way to increase emotional and physical closeness in a relationship, but sometimes it is difficult to develop a sex life that works for both partners. Part of the problem is that many people – particularly women – find it difficult to communicate what they really want in bed. A good way to become more assertive sexually is to take it in turns, in alternating love-making sessions, to be the active or passive partner.

As the active partner you take the initiative sexually while your partner gives you feedback about how your attentions make them feel. The passive partner comments on what is pleasurable and also gives guidance on how the active partner can improve their technique to make any less enjoyable experience better, for example, by adjusting the pressure of their touch or by focusing on a different part of the body.

As well as through physical contact, you can promote emotional closeness by being more open about your feelings. Think for a moment about how you express your love for your partner. Do you tell them you love them, or do you prefer to show your love through actions, such as running his or her bath every night? Try the following test. Each write a list of the ways in which you feel you demonstrate your love for your partner. Next swap lists and each assess whether the things your partner has noted actually make you feel loved. Then discuss your findings and each say how the other could more eloquently express their love.

exercise 9

BREATHING LIFE INTO LOVE

In many cultures the breath is seen as a manifestation of the spirit; and when we breathe together, it is thought that there is a communion of souls. This exercise will help you to harmonize your breathing so that you each develop a sense of unity with the other. Choose a quiet room in which to perform the exercise and play some quiet, meditative music to help you focus and relax. You will need a clock to time the session.

one
Partner A lies down on a bed or the floor, face up – they are the timekeeper. Partner B lies at right angles to Partner A, with their head resting on Partner A's stomach, as if on a pillow.

two
Both relax and slow down your breathing. Partner B now tries to synchronize their breathing exactly with Partner A's. Be attentive to what it feels like to breathe in harmony with your partner. Keep up the soft rhythm of mutual breathing for 5 minutes.

three
Change roles, so that Partner B is the timekeeper and Partner A rests their head on B's stomach. Partner A now matches their breathing to Partner B's for 5 minutes.

four
Compare notes on your experiences. Share with each other whether the exercise was difficult or easy for you, and what it felt like for your breathing to be in tune. Return to this exercise to recover closeness whenever you feel yourselves becoming distant.

strategy 2: appreciation

Knowing that we are appreciated can be the difference between being happy and being unhappy. The opposite side of the coin, of course, is being taken for granted, which nobody relishes: it is a kind of short-sightedness, a failure of imagination, as well as an injustice, and often makes the victim feel festering resentment.

Appreciation has two components: knowing the worth of your partner's character, talents, attitudes and behaviour; and expressing gratitude for that worth, and for the gestures, sometimes very small gestures, that embody it.

Partnerships sometimes move so far from appreciation that they settle down, on one side or both, to a habit of perpetual grumbling. If you feel that you have fallen into this trap, shake yourself out of it immediately. Stop complaining, and instead think of one truly positive thing to say. When you look at your relationship optimistically you will inspire not only your partner but also yourself. You will regain the energy and enthusiasm you were in danger of losing.

The key to appreciating your partner and your relationship is to begin to appreciate everything in your life. Allow small things to acquire their true value, and your relationship will naturally find its own rightful place high on the scale. Start to be aware of your surroundings, the sensations you experience. One of the easiest ways to appreciate simply being alive is to focus on your breathing, and in the process become more aware of your body and its connections with the outside world. Another good way to begin is by practising a smile. First, look in a mirror and try to

familiarize yourself with your habitual expression. Do you usually look cheerful or solemn? Now watch what happens if you let your face break into smile. Notice how this instantly lifts your mood. Make it your new practice to smile at your partner first thing in the morning and when you first greet them at the end of the working day. Then extend the practice of smiling to include everyone you meet.

If this "smile therapy" teaches us anything, it is that appreciation is an attitude with a narrow turning circle. You can move from indifference to involvement like flipping a coin in the head

*Appreciation is a
wonderful thing. It
makes what is excellent
in others belong
to us as well.*

Voltaire (1694–1778)

— and you have only to do this trick once to see how effective and rewarding it is. Begin in a small way. Look at your relationship and count your blessings. Ask yourself: "What can I be grateful for?" Perhaps the fact that you are able to travel together to work each day, or that your partner enjoys doing the ironing! Now consider specifically what is special about your partner? Try to see his or her full potential. Sit down and make a list of all the things you appreciate about this person whose path has crossed with yours. Some of these aspects might involve you, but some might not: perhaps your partner cares devotedly for an elderly relative, showing their capacity for compassion; perhaps he or she can make you laugh by doing impressions of people, demonstrating their humorous spontaneity; and so on.

Familiar aspects of a relationship tend to be treated eventually as a norm — which is hardly surprising when we have no other points of comparison. Our partner could be wittier, cleverer, kinder, sexier, more generous or more self-sacrificing than any one else with whom we might have formed a relationship, yet of course we have no concrete way to confirm this. We might be tempted to compare him or her with our friends' partners — perhaps we know someone among them who is more practical, or better educated, or more artistic — yet no real comparison is possible, because we can never know what these people are like to live with, or even just to be involved with. In any case, making comparisons is ungenerous and unnecessary. Better to acknowledge the unique combination of qualities in your partner, and make a conscious effort to show how much you value those qualities — by gestures both spoken and symbolic.

exercise 10

THE LOW-WHINE DIET

Many people habitually complain to their partner – it's time to break that habit and become more constructive about your relationship. The object of this exercise is to teach you how to cultivate a deeper appreciation of your loved one. Don't worry whether he or she appreciates you enough – just focus on your own unfolding sense of appreciation.

one
Observing the Low–Whine Diet entails refraining from criticizing your partner to his or her face, or to anyone else, for a week. You should both go on the diet at the same time, so pick a week together.

two
Establish a set of guidelines together – for example, you could include banning jokey put-downs and sarcasm. Name-calling, even in jest, is definitely out!

three
Notice when negative thoughts about your partner enter your mind, and silence them. A good way to do this is to think: "My partner may be difficult at times but he or she is also …", adding in a quality that you can appreciate. Now focus on that positive quality.

four
Each day, pay your partner a compliment or praise him or her in some way. (But make sure your comment is true and heartfelt, otherwise it will have no power.)

five
Look out for any small things that your partner does for you and express your appreciation for them. Make a point of thanking him or her, and give them a hug.

six
After the week has finished, compare notes with your partner and analyze how your levels of appreciation for each other have changed. You should find that by always focusing on the good points, your appreciation of one another has increased and that you have re-learned to notice what is special about your partner and your union.

strategy 3: compassion

Compassion for our fellow human beings is a cornerstone of many of the world's spiritual traditions. It is one of the great transformative human emotions because in showing compassion we transcend the constraints of our "self" and embrace a broader, more open-minded view of life that emphasizes human connectedness rather than individuality. This sense of kinship brings insight and healing both to ourselves and to the people toward whom we demonstrate compassion.

If our ultimate goal is to show compassion to everyone, we might assume that it would be easy to start with the person closest to us – our partner. Yet it is often easier to show compassion toward a complete stranger than toward the person we love most. When we see our partner suffering, we often respond with anxiety or frustration instead of compassion. This is because any suffering we see in our partner can trigger a fear of loss and a sense of helplessness in us. After all, our lives are intimately intertwined and we can be sure that whatever suffering our partner is experiencing will impinge on our own life as well. All these uncomfortable emotions, such as fear and resentment, can get in the way of feeling compassionate toward our partner. And yet it's vital to practise compassion in a relationship because it is the path to forgiveness and can be a lifeline for your partner in times of grief and pain.

We have already looked at the importance of empathy in a successful relationship (see pp.28–31) – the sense of being close to one's partner's innermost feelings, almost to the point of

mind-reading. Compassion is practical empathy in situations where help is needed. It takes the form of understanding your partner's problem, and being both sensitive in what you say and constructive in what you do. The technique of deep listening (see pp.110–17) can be a valuable part of the process.

The commitment to grow old together is a commitment to being compassionate through all the stages of aging. Even in the most fortunate lives there will be periods of grief and mourning, when compassion will be required. If your loved one is suffering, you may find that you are pulled in two different directions: on the one hand, you may feel an instinctive aversion to their anguish or pain and wish to turn away from it. On the other hand, you may find yourself wanting almost to embrace their suffering, to take on the burden and "make it better" for your partner. Think back to an occasion when your partner broke down in mental anguish – for example, on hearing of a bereavement – or endured severe physical pain. What was your response? If you find such suffering hard to face, remember that a simple way to steady yourself in a crisis is to focus on your breathing – centring yourself through breathing slowly and deeply will give you the strength to show your compassion when it is most needed.

A good way to enhance your compassion for yourself and your partner is to practise the Buddhist "loving kindness" medi-tation. Find somewhere quiet and sit comfortably in an upright posture. Now close your eyes and start by focusing on yourself with love and acceptance. You might like to say silently to yourself, "May I be well. May I be at peace." Try to let go of all your preoccupations, hopes and desires, and just "be". Accept that you are present, here and now, and feel wonder and gratitude for your existence. Now extend the same sense of loving kindness to encompass the life of your partner. Focus on them as a precious work of creation, a unique being whom you have the privilege to know. Embrace them in your heart with love and acceptance. You might like to use the words, "May you be well. May you be at peace," as you send them your heartfelt wishes for their wellbeing. Focus on their uniqueness, their positive qualities, and on the mystery of what it is that makes them themselves.

exercise 11

AWAKENING THE TENDER HEART

This exercise will help you and your partner develop the skill of identifying with each other's emotions by allowing you to experience, just for a moment, what life feels like for the other person. You will need a clock for time-keeping.

one
Choose somewhere where you will not be disturbed, such as a quiet room or a peaceful garden, and sit comfortably, opposite each other. You will take it in turns to be the speaker and the listener (who also acts as time-keeper). Toss a coin to determine who will speak first.

two
Pick an emotionally charged experience to recount – it should be something that happened outside your relationship and away from home. For example, perhaps you had a disagreement with a friend recently, and this made you feel angry and sad. Make sure that you talk primarily of your emotional reaction to the experience, rather than simply telling the story.

three
Swap seats. The listener now "becomes" the speaker and tries to reproduce, as closely as possible, what he or she just heard, reproducing not only the remembered words, but also the tone of voice and posture of the speaker. The idea is to induce in yourself the same emotions that your partner felt. Now, describe to your partner the feelings you experienced. Name the emotions and the order in which you felt them. How intense were they? If your partner thinks you were not notably successful at reproducing the emotions that they felt, keep trying to improve your ability to empathize.

four
When you have both had a turn as speaker and listener, reflect on how it felt to "be" your partner. Do you now feel more compassionate toward him or her? Discuss your findings with each other and suggest ways in which you can put what you have learned from this exercise into practice in your relationship.

strategy 4: honesty

Most people agree that honesty is important in a relationship, but very few couples are rigorously honest with each other. This doesn't necessarily mean that we plan to be deceitful, just that sometimes we think a conversation might be better tackled "at another time" or we feel slightly ashamed or embarrassed about something and would rather bury the issue than own up.

What holds people back from being totally honest is fear, and in a relationship this is primarily fear of losing our partner. In order to deal with this fear most people adapt their personality, at least to some degree, to please their partner and to make themselves more lovable. This is a form of dishonesty, like donning a mask. It then becomes a scary prospect to take off the mask and reveal your true self in your naked reality, with all your emotional responses laid bare.

It is often a long time before you feel that you can really open up to your partner and reveal your innermost feelings. This is because you are afraid to tell him or her things that you think they might find hard to accept. You can make a start by telling your partner honestly how you feel in a particular situation: "When you do X, I feel Y." As long as you confine yourself to expressing emotions, your partner is likely to listen without becoming defensive. After all, who can argue if you state, "I feel sad"? Bear in mind that if you introduce thoughts or opinions, you are open to challenge, and arguments can ensue.

Once you have started speaking honestly and you have built up a degree of trust with your partner in small things, you might

*The greatest happiness
of life is the conviction
that we are loved –
loved for ourselves,
or rather, loved in
spite of ourselves.*

Victor Hugo (1802–1885)

feel ready to confide in them over more serious matters. Perhaps you have a secret (such as having had an affair, or possessing a criminal record), and you fear that divulging it will sabotage your relationship. It takes great courage to speak the truth, because you might hurt your partner deeply and you cannot predict the outcome. So before you reveal all, take a moment to question your motive. Are you sure that you are being honest in order to improve your relationship? Or are you doing so to rid yourself of a long-held burden and so make yourself feel better? If you are certain that you are telling your partner the truth in the interests

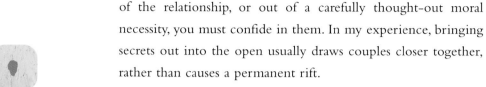

of the relationship, or out of a carefully thought-out moral necessity, you must confide in them. In my experience, bringing secrets out into the open usually draws couples closer together, rather than causes a permanent rift.

At the other extreme from keeping secrets, we can find ourselves being dishonest in small ways, such as telling "little white lies" that we might feel do no real harm. The problem with this is that even small acts of dishonesty can lead to a breakdown in trust. By way of illustration, suppose you splashed out on an expensive suit, spending money that you had agreed you would save. Because you feel guilty, you tell your partner that the clothes were a bargain. But they discover the truth when, for once, they happen to come across the bill you have filed away, and they are hurt, not because you spent the money, but because you lied. It is always better to own up if we let our partner down, rather than risk undermining their trust in us by compounding our aberration with a lie.

Another important aspect of honesty is our ability to say "no". Sometimes in a relationship the more placid partner might find themselves going along with their partner's wishes just to keep the peace. But suppressing your own desires in this way builds resentment and erodes love. Remember, you can't readily change your partner, but you *can* change how you respond to them. Asserting yourself and saying "no" to what you don't want is important – it means you are honouring your own integrity. And if you can both be honest about what you like and dislike, you will find life easier, because you will both know precisely where you stand. Now try the exercise opposite.

exercise 12

TRUTH-SAYING

This exercise will help you practise the skill of speaking the honest truth. Arrange to perform it when you are relaxed and are getting on well together. Take as a theme a disagreement you had in the past that is apparently resolved but that still produces an undercurrent of tension between you.

one
Sit side by side. You will be taking it in turns to be the speaker and the listener. Toss a coin to see who goes first as the speaker. Decide which disagreement you will use and both resolve to approach it with an open mind.

two
The first speaker starts by speaking of his or her experience, mentioning only their own emotions, without blaming the partner. Start by using the formula: "When you … , I felt … ." Take 5 minutes to describe your feelings. Then allow yourself to access a deeper level of emotions by saying: "Really, deep down, I felt … ." For example, if you were angry, now speak of the hurt, disappointment or fear that was beneath your anger.

three
Swap roles and listen to your partner's experience of the same argument.

four
When you have both had a turn at being speaker and listener, ask yourselves how you now feel about the disagreement. Discuss what you have each learned from hearing the honest truth. How can this knowledge help you resolve other ongoing disputes?

strategy 5: dialogue

It takes effort and discipline to learn the skills of constructive dialogue, which lie at the heart of any successful relationship. The rewards, however, are inestimable – each time you approach a difficult conversation with honesty, kindness, respect, empathy and imagination, you are taking steps to strengthen the bond of your partnership.

The two key skills of constructive dialogue are "deep listening" and straight talking. Deep listening means stilling your own mental chatter, banishing any preconceived judgments or defensive thoughts and focusing entirely on what your partner has to say. The more you become absorbed in listening, the more insights you gather.

You might think that you are already a good listener, but you can still benefit from the following deep listening techniques. Begin practising in small ways. When someone is speaking to you, resist the urge to respond before they have completed their say. If you find yourself formulating answers before they have finished talking, let go of your thoughts and refocus on what you hear.

Another good way to train yourself in deep listening is, when you are alone, to close your eyes and home in on the sounds around you: traffic noise, birdsong, the radio – anything. Try to stretch your listening abilities by picking out one sound and allowing it to fill your consciousness. If your mind wanders, bring it gently back to the sound. Now apply the same technique when you listen to your partner. Focus on their voice alone and

It takes two to speak
the truth: one to speak,
and another to hear.

Henry David Thoreau
(1817–1862)

consciously try to stay tuned in. Concentrate your mind and listen carefully to what your partner actually says. Try to stop yourself interpreting any underlying meanings; instead, accept the words at face value. If you are unsure that you have grasped their correct meaning, repeat back what you've heard in your own words – checking that you've understood properly can prevent misunderstandings from arising later. When your partner has finished speaking, don't rush to reply immediately. Give yourself a few moments to digest the totality of what has been said before formulating a response.

Tuning in to your partner is only half the equation: the other half is developing the ability to express yourself truthfully and wisely. You can start by ensuring that you say exactly what you mean. For example, if you are upset, maybe because your partner is unable to attend a family celebration, tell him or her! If instead you say that you don't mind, they are unlikely to guess how you really feel and are therefore unlikely to do anything about it. Then you might find yourself resenting them and, if you repeat this behaviour over time, your relationship will suffer.

Another way to talk effectively with your partner is to refrain from using language that blames him or her. Take responsibility for your own actions and feelings by using "I"-statements, not "you"-statements. For example, say to your partner: "I didn't really enjoy the movie, but that's my fault for not realizing that it was an action film," instead of "You know I don't enjoy action films, so why did you choose one?" By approaching the matter in this way you speak truthfully of your own experience, yet you avoid putting your partner on the defensive.

It is also easy to fall into the trap of nagging your partner, which is likely to make them simply "switch off" and not listen. Try to avoid using terms such as "always" or "never"; for example, rather than say: "You never do the dishes", try: "I'd appreciate some help with the dishes. Why don't you wash and I'll dry?" By making a constructive suggestion in this way you encourage your partner to respond favourably. You open, rather than close, communication. If you would like to work more on dialogue, perform the exercise opposite and then see strategies 2: Appreciation (pp.98–101) and 4: Honesty (pp.106–109).

exercise 13

WALKING IN THE OTHER'S SHOES

*In this exercise you test both your listening and speaking skills. By each
taking turns at listening and speaking and both summarizing what you feel are the salient
points of each talk, you will be able to see at a glance how well you are communicating.
You will need a clock for timing and two pens and some paper for writing.*

one
Toss a coin to determine who will speak first. The speaker
then chooses a subject that is not connected with the relationship and talks about it
for 5 minutes. You could perhaps recount a journey or tell your partner how you spent
your day, but make sure you mention things you enjoyed or disliked doing, anything you
found particularly interesting or dull, and so on, to make the talk lively.

two
When the speaker has finished, take a pen and piece of paper and each write down what
you consider to be the five most important points made by the speaker.
Now put the papers aside.

three
Swap roles so that the first speaker now becomes the listener and the first listener
becomes the speaker. Again, the speaker talks for 5 minutes on a subject unrelated to the
relationship. Then you both summarize on paper the five most important points
in the second talk.

four
Now compare the points you each wrote down for each talk. How well do you think your
partner listened to you and vice versa? Did you both pick out the same five things? Were
you a better speaker or listener? Discuss ways in which you could use this technique
to improve your communication skills within the relationship.

Once you have improved your dialogue skills you can apply them constructively to the art of problem-solving. But before we look at ways of solving problems together, let's get one thing clear: sweeping them under the rug is not the answer! Problem-solving is cathartic. Even when the solution is difficult or apparently undesirable, finding it is fundamental to our own peace of mind and to the positive dynamics of our relationship.

Within a relationship our own understanding of the problem can become blurred by the feelings of our partner, whose view might be very different from our own. Working at a situation together is not like recruiting a friend to help you with a personal problem of your own. Yes, you need your partner's help in solving the problem, and he or she will need yours, but what this means in practice is an agreement to work together in a spirit of mutual understanding and cooperation. Above all, you both need to be prepared to talk – or to postpone talking for a while if you hit an impasse, or feel that the discussion is going round in circles, or if one of you feels emotionally drained.

The first step is to sit down together and discuss whether you both agree that a problem exists. Often within a relationship one partner will consider something to be wrong, while the other thinks that everything is fine. When one of you thinks there is a problem, the other must let him or her have their say – remember, the emotions that you each experience are equally valid, even if they aren't shared. Resolve before you start that you will find a solution together.

The next step is for each of you to write down your own view of the problem in one or two sentences. Then, each write down

two possible solutions. You may be able to think of more, but be strict with yourself and pick your best two solutions.

Next, each of you should read out your sentences identifying the problem. How do your analyses differ? Even at this early stage arguments can occur, so be disciplined. Concentrate solely on definitions, do not be tempted to stray into solutions yet. Avoid interrupting each other, instead, wait until the other has finished a particular point. It can help to agree on some ground-rules beforehand. For example, if either of you has a particular point to make in response to what is being said, you raise your hand; the other person then finishes outlining his or her

We have two ears and one mouth so that we can listen twice as much as we speak.

Epictetus (c.55–135CE)

particular point but allows you your say before launching upon any new ideas. Keep your voices level and calm. Hold hands while you talk, as a gesture of loving cooperation.

Once you have defined the problem together, each of you should read silently through your possible solutions – and, if you wish, modify them in the light of the conversation you have just had – before reading them aloud. As you listen to what your partner has to say, monitor your feelings. If you find yourself bridling, or feeling panicky, ask yourself whether this is a valid reaction to what is being proposed. Try to step back mentally from the predicament, and look at it in a long perspective. We all have a tendency to react to hypothetical ideas as if they were real situations: our imaginations, which help us to evaluate ideas, can also clothe them in terror. But just keep reminding yourself that a suggestion is just a suggestion, that the outcome of your dialogue will be something you work out together, not the preliminary thoughts that you hear from your partner.

After exchanging your prepared solutions, exchange your initial reactions – is there anything on which you agree? If not, don't worry! We often become so bogged down in a problem that it inhibits our creativity – our ability to find imaginative, mutually satisfactory solutions. To unlock your creativity, you need to get away from your preoccupation with the problem and clear your mind. Leave the room and do something relaxing and enjoyable. Try to make it a joint activity – taking a long walk or having a picnic. When you are ready, sit somewhere quiet together and prepare to brainstorm solutions. The exercise opposite suggests how you might approach this.

exercise 14

THE ORDERLY CHAOS MIND MAP®

In this exercise you draw a Mind Map®, which you can use to create an overview of your relationship. The suggestions below describe a Mind Map® of your whole relationship, but you can adapt them to cover the particular area of your bond that needs attention.

one
Take a large sheet of paper and some coloured pens. Either draw two hearts or two people or write the word "Relationship" in large letters in the middle of the page.

two
Next, draw seven broad wavy lines extending out like branches on a tree around the central image or word. Make each line a different colour. Name them in bold letters: Commitment, Intimacy, Passion, Interests, Freedom, Finances and Chores.

three
Near the end of each of the seven broad lines (and keeping to the same colours), draw two or more "branches", depending on how many you feel you need to add. For example, on the "Commitment" line, you might like to have branches labelled: "Time"; "Future goals"; "Fidelity"; and so on.

four
Now add some extra "twigs", branching out from each line. For example, you could have "Getting married or living together" coming out from the "Future goals" line. Then do the same with all the other lines, developing the branches outward as far as you can. When you have finished, you will have a complete overview of your relationship.

five
Analyze your Mind Map® and pinpoint problem areas to discuss with your partner.

six
Compare and discuss each map in turn. Then, draw a new map that reflects both points of agreement and common areas of concern. Now begin your dialogue to find mutually satisfactory solutions.

strategy 6: vision

Most couples embark on a relationship without first finding out whether they have a common dream or vision of the future. Of course, they exchange views in a general way on topics such as marriage, career ambitions and so on – this is all part of the ongoing process of getting to know each other. But in the early stages of a relationship we tend to avoid discussing weighty matters, either for fear of scaring off our partner or possibly out of some deep-rooted belief that lightheadedness is the mood of love. This means that sometimes we make assumptions about our partner's stance on a particular topic, only to be shocked later when we discover that their opinions on, say, how to bring up children are the antithesis of our own. While any small disparities in your visions for the future can be easily worked through, fundamental differences might prove insurmountable. It is therefore important as early as possible in the relationship to find out whether your visions are compatible with each other.

As the partnership matures, from time to time you still need to monitor that you are both headed in the same direction. Otherwise two close partners can turn into two loosely connected strangers. To dream of a new future together and to work hard to make that come true develops a special unity of purpose. When you help each other to realize your dream, you become an invincible team. And indeed, when you make a serious commitment to achieve that vision by setting and writing down goals and allowing others to witness your pledge, your vision becomes activated – as you grow together, you grow your dream.

Visions, of course, don't just happen. Nor does entertaining a vision, even if it is imagined in considerable detail, take us any closer to its realization. While we sit back, comfortable in our daily routine, nothing much changes. We have to make our visions come true by working toward them. In so doing we become a magnet that attracts opportunities to help us achieve our goals. But of course our dreams need to be realistic – there's no point in setting your heart on becoming an opera star if you are tone-deaf (although you might choose to take singing lessons to improve your ear).

*Grow old
along with me,
The best is
yet to be.*

Robert Browning
(1812–1889)

To shape your relationship successfully, you need to have a vision of where you wish to be, both individually and as a couple, within a set timescale. You could start by defining exactly what each of you means by "the future" – you might be thinking in terms of years, whereas your partner might feel that next month is a sufficiently distant horizon. Bear in mind that you will need to give yourselves a realistic amount of time in which to achieve your vision, but not so much time that achievement seems an unreal prospect. Certainly, a plan that takes from three to five years sounds perfectly credible.

Start by envisaging your ideal future (it's never too late to do this, even if you are just beginning your retirement). Consider the practical details, such as where you would like to live: perhaps in a city? in the countryside? or somewhere more unusual, such as on a boat? If you don't already have children, do you want them? If so, how many? What are the things you would like to do together? How much time do you wish to spend together? How much time alone? And so on. Now think of your personal dreams and see how those fit in with your vision for your future as a couple.

When you have worked out both your mutual vision and your personal dreams, write a note of commitment: "We will ... by the year ..." and sign it. The next step is to ask one of your friends to countersign it as a witness. This helps emphasize the seriousness of your intentions. When you have completed these steps, you have activated your dream plan and events will begin to align themselves around your vision.

Now ask yourself what the first small step toward realizing your vision should be, and then do the exercise opposite, which will show you how to maintain focus on your goal.

exercise 15

SYMPATHETIC MAGIC

This exercise will help you and your partner realize your short-term visions for your future together. The idea is that you both write down your dreams in a "Visions Book". Then, together you choose one at random and discuss how to make that dream – for example, to take an exotic holiday in six months' time – a reality. To use as your "Visions Book" you will need a small notebook, which you should keep where you can both easily find it.

one
Whenever either of you is inspired with a dream, write it down in your "Visions Book".

two
Every month one of you selects a vision from your book, which you then discuss to help you decide whether you really wish to make it a reality. (If you don't, cross it out, and choose another one from your book until you find a dream that you both want.)

three
Now start to create your dream by choosing something to represent it and put this object in a place where you will be constantly reminded of your goal. For example, if you wish to go on an exotic holiday, you might put a colourful shell on your dressing table. Or, if you have set your hearts on finding a new apartment, put an old front-door key on your living-room coffee table. Creating a symbolic representation of your dream and repeatedly focusing on it sends out positive energy which, like a magnet, attracts the conditions that will make your dream come true.

four
Monitor your progress at monthly intervals and once you feel happy that your first goal is within sight, you can take another dream suggestion from your "Vision Book", and start to focus on realizing that dream too.

strategy 7: time

Time, in an important sense, is the medium in which a relationship exists. We spend time with each other, at home where we tend to measure time by weekends, and on vacation where every day is equally precious; and we spend time apart. Our lives are a series of goodbyes and reunions, endlessly alternating. We age together imperceptibly, and mark the stages of our aging in a string of birthdays, usually acknowledged (by special meals or gatherings and the giving of presents) if not exactly celebrated.

All this suggests a passive relationship with time, a surrender to its inexorable flow. However, we are all familiar these days with the concept of time management, by which, in the workplace, we take time in hand and make it serve us as much as possible. In relationships, too, a form of time management can be beneficial. For example, if your relationship is floundering through sheer inertia, you need to start spending more quality time together to reinforce your bond. Or one or both of you might lead such complicated lives, owing to work or family circumstances, that you need consciously to forge interludes of time in which to be together at all. But the truth is that every couple can benefit from an audit of their time, distinguishing, for example, between quality time spent together, routine time spent together, time spent apart in the interest of the common good, and time voluntarily spent apart.

One helpful starting-point for making an assessment is to keep a Time Journal for a week, in which you and your partner each record what you did each day, from waking to bedtime. Mark in

your waking and sleeping hours, and divide the former into the following categories: solitary time, household chores, family or childcare duties, socializing, sport or recreation, creative activity, sacred time and "couple" time (just being together and talking), noting (in all but the first and last categories, which are self-explanatory) whether you did this with your partner or alone.

At the end of the week add up the total amount of waking time you spent together each day outside working hours, and the total spent alone or with others. How do the two compare? Discuss what you feel would be a healthy balance – this is very much a matter for each couple to determine themselves, but as a guide (not a prescription!) you might aim to spend fifty per cent of your spare time together, fifty per cent pursuing individual interests. If work robs you of "couple time", see if you can adopt more flexible working hours and so gain more time with your partner.

Now look at the time that you already spend together. Do you use it constructively to nurture the relationship? When doing chores together, do you regard this as pure duty, or do you also derive pleasure from being together? Resolve to put aside set periods in which you discuss serious matters such as finances, family problems and so on, so that you can spend the rest of your time together simply enjoying each other's company. Next, look at the time you spend following individual interests. Ask yourself if you could involve your partner in these, so that you could spend more quality time with each other. For example, could they come along to your exercise class? Could you give them a rewarding role on one of your creative projects? How about sacred time? – could you meditate or pray together? And so on.

Some people practise some form of relationship time management during ordinary time but neglect it during vacations – after all, why worry about the quality of time when the burden of work is lifted? In fact, however, even vacations benefit from careful planning and a balance of solo time and time spent together. And if time for discussing serious issues (for example, the state of your relationship) has been limited before the vacation, try not to let the unresolved concerns dominate too much of your break: any such discussions are best tackled in the mornings, so that the rest of the day, and the precious evenings, are free.

exercise 16

HEART HOUR

*Setting aside a regular time to reconnect with your partner is crucial to a successful
relationship. Try to find time each week to spend one "Heart Hour" together. This is
a time to reflect, to heal wounds and to pour energy into your relationship. Try to
arrange your "Heart Hour" at a time when you can both relax in peaceful
surroundings. You will need a clock with an alarm, and you may find it
helpful to play some meditative background music.*

one
Set the alarm to sound after 5 minutes. Now, start with the "Soul Gaze". Sit close together,
facing each other. Then look into each other's eyes and hold a soft, steady gaze. Keep
completely silent during this time, even if you feel awkward or giggly. Notice your
bodily sensations and any emotions you feel.

two
When the alarm sounds, end the "Soul Gaze" by hugging your partner. Share with
each other how you felt during the "Soul Gaze".

three
Now review the time you spent together during the past week. Consider your
experiences together. What went well? What was enjoyable and fruitful? What
did you find difficult? Use constructive questions, such as, "What could we
do differently next time?", or, "What would help you now?"

four
Choose one of your favourite exercises from this book and complete it.

strategy 8: freedom

Freedom can be a touchy issue, even in the best of relationships, because commitment really does lead to a voluntary restriction of liberty. Even when our love for our partner is strong, there is a part of us that still hankers after that perfect freedom we remember delighting in when we were single. Sometimes this can cause us to resent our present restrictions and the freedom our partner seems to be enjoying, and we find ourselves making jokes or little digs when they pursue their interests or spend time with their own friends. Such resentment can be a sign of niggling jealousy or of a sense of injustice because we perceive that our partner has more freedom than we have. Worse still, people in unhealthy relationships can feel trapped or even imprisoned – although they know that the relationship is not good for them, their fear of loneliness, of violence or of their children suffering if the relationship fails is so great that they feel helpless to act.

However, freedom – in the most important sense of the word – is something that any healthy relationship allows to both parties, and is by no means incompatible with commitment. Some relationships, it is true, impose restrictions implictly: without any discussion taking place, it is somehow understood that certain independent initiatives are unacceptable – perhaps because both parties feel that the only life they have is the life they share. If, as you read this, you recognize the truth of the description, there is probably an issue in your partnership that needs to be addressed.

Some couples live in a house of mirrors: when they look out into the world, they see only each other. It can be revealing to

We need in love to
practise only this:
letting each other go.
For holding on comes
easily – we do not need
to learn it.

**Rainer Maria Rilke
(1875–1926)**

do a visualization based on this image. Think of yourself as living in a house with mirror-lined walls: you see your partner and yourself sitting on a sofa together. But one day the silvered back of the mirror starts to fade, and the reflective surfaces gradually become clear. What do you perceive through these walls of glass? What life do you see for yourself beyond your relationship? Do you observe yourself pursuing independent interests, or is this merely wish-fulfilment? Many people believe that they live in a glass prison but in fact they have the magical ability to walk through the walls.

If there seems to be a set of rules in your relationship about what you should or shouldn't do, you might like to look together at who makes and who follows these rules. Sometimes relationships can get stuck in a restrictive pattern of relating. When this happens, you need to discuss how to break the impasse. One way to broach the topic might be to start with a unilateral declaration: "If you'd like to do a residential painting course one day, you could." Or you could phrase it as a question: "Have you ever thought of ... ?" You might then go on to itemize some of the practical ways in which you could make such a break possible – which might involve taking on some of your partner's commitments while he or she is away. Then, after an appropriate interval, outline your own wish for constructive freedom, letting your partner know how you would like to pursue *your* interests.

One reason why some people restrict their own freedom within a relationship is that, while outwardly they yearn for freedom, inwardly they enjoy the safety of their "cage". They themselves hold the key but are too timid to unlock the door and walk outside. If this characterization rings true for you, now is the time to act. There is no point in waiting for your partner to "give" you your freedom: you are a slave only to your own fears. Freedom is an important factor in any relationship, and one that brings great benefits to both parties – not least because time spent apart helps you to recharge your batteries and brings an influx of positive energy both of you can enjoy. But in the most successful bonds, freedom is handled with both fairness and consideration. Ask, even when you feel you need no permission; negotiate, even when you feel you have an absolute right.

exercise 17

THE ELASTICITY CHALLENGE

In this exercise, you investigate the balance of freedom versus control in your relationship. Take turns to speak and listen, tossing a coin to determine who goes first. Be considerate toward each other and bear in mind that the wish to control is caused by fear. You will need a clock to time yourselves.

one
Sit side by side, holding hands. The speaker has 5 minutes to talk. He or she starts by saying, "If I had more freedom, I would like to …" They then mention one cherished (and not impossible) dream and one milder ambition (the advantage of this is that conversation can focus on the lesser dream if the major one proves to be too difficult to talk about). The speaker then talks about what these freedoms would mean to him or her.

two
Then both of you spend 1 minute silently thinking through what was said.

three
The listener then comments freely on his or her reaction to the partner's wishes. The reaction might be emotional – for example, a feeling of panic, anger or sadness. It is important to be honest about any such response. Fears, in particular, should be freely aired. The listener should then say which of the two mentioned freedoms they feel they could accommodate in part or in full.

four
Swap roles.

five
After you have completed this exercise, each partner has the option to exercise freedom under the agreed terms – subject to an agreed period of notice. The value of the exercise is that it allows you both plenty of time to explore and think about the freedoms desired before they progress to being concrete plans.

strategy 9: play

Play brightens our life and gladdens our heart. It is a source of happiness, excitement, relaxation. And yet adults tend to lose their ability to play, becoming more and more serious and set in their ways as they age. So where does all our playfulness go when we reach adulthood? Sadly, it is often completely buried under the ever-increasing burden of responsibilities. Sometimes playfulness resurfaces temporarily during courtship, when we display our most attractive behaviour to charm our partner. But once the relationship matures, our urge to play often recedes again.

Watch any group of children totally immersed in play – there is something wonderful and heartwarming in their happy, laughing chatter. Let's take a closer look at *how* they play. Imagine they are building a sandcastle on the beach. They are active, making walls and digging dams. They are also creative, taking pleasure in the freedom to fashion the sand to their own design. While they play, the children interact closely, completely absorbed in their task. Their excitement and energy grow in anticipation of completing their masterpieces. Above all they are having fun. From this example we can see that the main elements of play are creativity, freedom, spontaneity, companionship, excitement, energy and fun.

If only we, as adults, can learn to recapture a little of this playful exuberance, we can reintroduce lightheartedness into our relationship. Of course, play means different things to different people, but in general it can be defined as something we do out of sheer exuberance and for no other reason. When you play

with your partner, you can temporarily shed your responsibilities and act as if you have no cares. You can step out of the circle of serious issues in which you occupy a central position. And, of course, you can sidestep your predominant mood and pass into a state of pure enjoyment.

Think for a moment: do you and your partner ever play together? Do you spend time together with the sole aim of enjoying yourselves? Participating in sports, games and dancing are all types of play, but another, no less rewarding, is a witty, free-wheeling, gossipy, spontaneous exchange of conversation, peppered with humour. Perhaps you think, "But my life is so busy,

To laugh often and to love much ... to appreciate beauty, to find the best in others, to give one's self ... this is to have succeeded.

Ralph Waldo Emerson
(1803–1882)

I can't afford the time to play." Well, I say that you can't afford to be without play! It is beneficial both physically and mentally because it releases tension and stress. Play helps you to stay healthy by promoting wellbeing.

No matter how busy you are, resolve to make time to play. Plan some playtime together. Often a good opportunity is an unusual adventure of some kind – a fairground ride, a walk to a ruined house, a boat trip, a visit by elevator to the viewing gallery of a skyscraper. The possibilities are endless. If you are not spending at least a couple of hours per week on play, you are seriously missing out on something good for your relationship.

Do not worry if your partner is of a more serious cast of mind than yourself – your own spirit of playfulness may well become infectious. Conversely, if you find that your partner gets into the mood faster than you can, making you feel somewhat inhibited initially, that is no cause for concern – just relax and behave naturally. You are *allowed* to respond differently, so there is no problem if your own response to play is more subdued. Don't be inhibited by the constraints of society – dismiss comments from the critical commentator in your mind, such as "Act your age!" or "Don't make a fool of yourself!"

Of course, bedtime is the perfect opportunity for play, and most couples enjoy being on the boundary line between humour and passion. The smiles, the laughter – even the jokes – are all part of the sexual experience. Once we have accepted the idea of the bedroom as a playroom, we might start to think about other rooms in this context – the kitchen, for example. Why should not cooking, or even doing the dishes, be a playful interlude?

exercise 18

PLAY DAY

This exercise will help you experience different modes of play. The idea is that each partner take turns in planning a "Play Day". The activities you choose should appeal broadly to your partner, but at the same time may offer them a challenge. Don't discuss your ideas, try to keep your plans secret until the actual day. Toss a coin to determine who will be the first planner.

one
Try to choose pursuits that contrast with your partner's usual activities. For example, if you live in an urban area, you might plan to go somewhere rural on a horse trek or take a raft on a river, and so on. Or, if you live in the country, you might go into town to visit a museum or art gallery, or attend a rock concert. The only limitation is your imagination. However, do make sure that you arrange something that you know your partner will enjoy – there is no point in taking them, say, to the races if they hate crowds!

two
During your Play Day, allow yourselves to be spontaneous. Don't stick to a set timetable or do something, such as eat at a certain time, purely out of habit. If you feel like having lunch at 11am, then do so! And if your partner is enjoying a particular activity – say, a boat trip – and he or she would like to spend more time afloat than you had planned, just relax and go with the flow. Remember, the purpose of the day is not to follow a schedule but to forget all your worries and responsibilities and have fun together.

three
After you return, ask your partner for feedback about the Play Day. What did they like most about it? Was there anything that you could have done differently to make it more enjoyable for them? Bear this information in mind when it is your turn to organize the Play Day again.

strategy 10: surprise

In any relationship, over time, you can establish certain routines that make life run smoothly for both of you. This gives your partnership order and stability. But human nature being as it is, stability can soon be perceived as predictability, and before you know it you are bored and stuck in a rut. When you feel that your relationship has become a habit, the strategy to adopt is surprise. By re-introducing an element of unpredictability back into your life together, you can help to regain your sense of fun and revitalize the bond you share.

A good starting-point is to think back to when you first met and fell in love. Can you recall some of the spontaneous, maybe even crazy things you did to surprise your partner then? Perhaps one night at the seaside you stripped down to your underwear and went swimming; or perhaps, after an unexpected snowfall one winter's night, you got up early and built your partner a huge snowman. Use your memories as a springboard for ideas. There is no need to try to re-create past surprises (although, if you can remember a particular surprise that your partner loved – say, an exciting flight in a hot-air balloon – you might arrange for them to go on a similar flight in a different place). And of course, your surprise doesn't need to be extraordinary – you could organize a night out to see a play or a movie, or a night in together to watch a favourite video with a glass of your favourite wine or a box of chocolates. The important thing is to give your partner a surprise that breaks them out of their usual routine by doing something different and enjoyable.

Surprise parties are another fun way to bring excitement into your relationship. You don't need a special occasion in order to hold a celebration for your partner – in fact, if there is no particular reason for the party, it will be all the more of a surprise!

Giving flowers is another time-honoured and effective way of surprising your partner, especially if you put some thought into how you present them. For example, you could have them delivered to his or her office; or you could place them romantically on the bed; or you could hide them somewhere and leave a note with a clue as to where to find them. Put a message in with them – whether tender or witty, it can only augment the surprise.

Traditionally, we offer gifts on birthdays, anniversaries and festive days. But in fact, giving your partner a little present at any time of the year is a lovely way in which to surprise them and reinforce your love bond. Choose imaginative but inexpensive items (a single flower left on their pillow is enough) so that your partner doesn't feel pressured to return the gesture. The secret of finding the right things is to know your partner's tastes. Listen carefully to throwaway remarks which hint at his or her preferences; and write them down, or you are sure to forget.

A gift that shows inventiveness will often be more welcome than one that is merely costly. Into an attactive gift box you might put a number of items, related to each other by a common theme. For example, with a volume of Lord Byron's letters from Venice you might put a toy carnival mask, some handmade Italian notepaper and a high-quality pen. The linking theme could be something private that only your partner would be able to interpret. The advantage of this kind of multiple present is that you can include one inexpensive frivolous (indeed totally useless) item without detracting from the overall appeal of the package.

You might also introduce small surprises by leaving little notes to your partner around the home. For example, you could attach a note containing a loving or a humorous message to the bathroom mirror. Try to leave notes in places where your partner will least expect to find them, such as on the car dashboard, above the kitchen sink, inside their sock drawer, and so on. You might also like to show your partner your appreciation by sending him or her a postcard in the mail or an email, or by leaving them a personal message on their voice-mail.

exercise 19

A ROYAL EVENING

Take it in turns to offer your partner a surprise evening out. Make sure that you agree to a budget and stick within it. Try to make this surprise outing a monthly event.

one
Plan the evening, making sure that it is geared around your partner's interests. Imagine that he or she is royalty and that you are doing your utmost to please and entertain them. Give your partner the minimum of necessary information, such as how to dress for the occasion and at what time the evening is planned to start and finish. The organizer takes responsibility for arranging childcare, transport or any other practicalities so that the "royal" guest can just sit back and enjoy their treat.

two
Be imaginative in your choice of entertainment. You might find it helpful to keep a list of ideas, writing down each one as it comes to you. Perhaps you could organize a moonlight picnic on the beach, a visit to the cinema to see a film that he or she has long wanted to see, an romantic meal in a cosy little restaurant, or a trip to a fun-fair – the list of possible treats is endless.

three
Once you return home you can bring the evening to a relaxing close by laying on soft music, candlelight, a massage or whatever else would make your partner feel really pampered.

four
Next day, discuss the evening with your partner and find out what were the parts they they enjoyed most. Use this information to refine your next effort.

widening the network

Many of the approaches that improve the intimate bond of love can also benefit your relationships with family, friends and colleagues. A satisfying life is one surrounded by warm, heartfelt connections. However, to shape and maintain good relationships requires skills as well as effort.

It can be difficult to maintain continuous good relations with close family, such as parents and children, because as life progresses the relationship dynamics constantly shift. And when you are in a loving relationship, there is a risk of neglecting some of your friends. However, friendship is one of life's most valuable resources, as well as a way to introduce variety and balance into your routines. Relationships with colleagues are also important, if only because we spend such a large part of our lives at work.

This chapter presents effective methods to enhance your whole network of relationships outside the love bond.

family

What we are expected to take from, and what to give to family relationships varies from one culture to another. In some traditions, for example, high status is attributed to grandparents, who are seen not only as helping with childcare but also as an invaluable source of wisdom. Despite such cultural variations of emphasis there are common problems that seem to affect many families in the Western world – such as siblings in rivalry for their parents' love, children embroiled in the break-up of the parental bond, and adults coming to terms with abuse they received as children. It is also not uncommon to be caught in the cross-fire between partner and parent, or even to find oneself torn between conflicting loyalties. Most love relationships will not thrive in such circumstances.

When dealing with your own parents, be sensitive to the fact that their greatest fear is likely to be loss of your love. This means that you can negotiate new arrangements, when you have to, from a position of strength, with a view to creating a basis for a peaceful future. However, it is important to understand how they feel – to empathize with them. Never forget that one day you will be their age, and may share many of the responses they are experiencing now. Do not fall into the trap of believing that the happiness of the younger generation takes precedence over that of the older. Having to provide (perhaps not always financially, but certainly in terms of your time and effort) for parents who need nursing care, or just your company on a regular basis, can place a strain on love relationships, but any partner who truly

The diversity of the family should be a cause of love and harmony, as it is in music where many different notes blend together in the making of a perfect chord.

From the
Baha'i scriptures

loves you will understand how vital it is to return your parents' love to the best of your ability. After all, you are their main link to life's continuation, and that gives you an important place in their emotional landscape.

Of course, even with beloved parents you may need to assert your own individual needs, and this is even more likely in the case of in-laws (whether literally defined, if you are married, or more loosely, if you are not). A fundamental rule is that although you can't change the behaviour of others, you can change the way you relate to them. It is useful to dwell on this as you tackle any problems with one or both of your partner's parents, or perhaps with a difficult sibling or step-child. Sometimes you might be tempted to submit to uncomfortable situations just to keep the peace. However, being submissive seldom has this outcome! Check out your own feelings on the matter. If you feel resentment, this is a warning signal that you need to reset your boundaries if you are to avoid the risk of your love being corroded. Staying away from family gatherings might be preferable to suffering the damage they can cause. Try to be courteous in any encounters, and do not criticize your loved one's family in conversations with him or her. A positive approach of this kind will make it easier for you to reach a compromise.

Defining your "rules" about family behaviour in the light of your relationship and of your own personal needs and preferences might cause some hurt initially, but in the long run you will have more peace because everyone knows where they stand.

Outside these situations that involve both your relationship and the family networks that intersect with that relationship, there are, of course, many difficulties that can arise within a family; indeed, they are far too various and familiar to enumerate here, including conflicts over aspirations, lifestyle, character, attitude, behaviour, and much else besides. Much of the advice given in this book about the love bond can be applied, with appropriate adaptations, to blood ties – with the difference that blood ties cannot be so readily replaced if relations break down. Try to think of the involuntary aspect of the blood tie in a positive light: you share a spiritual link with this person, which means that it is worth investing a great deal of energy in getting on together; and you can reach out and touch each other in pure love, uncomplicated by romance.

exercise 20

THE RELATIONSHIP TREE

This exercise will help you obtain an overview of the dynamics of your relationships and give you information that will help you to set clear boundaries for acceptable behaviour. You will need a large sheet of paper and some coloured pens.

one
In the middle of the page draw a symbol to represent yourself – for example, you might draw the sun, or a flower, or something more abstract such as two or three concentric circles, or a triangle in a circle.

two
Now, using different colours to represent the various types of relationship you have, write the names (or if you prefer, draw symbols) of the people who are important in your life. Place each one at a distance from you that reflects the closeness of your relationship, and draw a connecting line between you; if the relationship is difficult, draw a broken line; if the bond is strong, draw a continuous line. Indicate the nature of your connection in words or using your own symbolic code.

three
Using a different coloured pen, add to your relationship tree any people who were once important to you, but with whom you are no longer in contact, such as an influential teacher, or a deceased relative, or a friend who has moved abroad. There may be some unresolved issues between you, in which case join yourself to them with a broken line.

four
Now draw appropriate interconnecting lines between the people on your diagram. For example, if your best friend gets on well with your brother, join them up with a bold, strong line. If your partner does not get on well with your father, draw a broken line.

five
When you have finished, put the relationship tree on the floor and close your eyes for a moment. Then take a fresh look at it. Analyze the trouble spots and think how you could overcome the conflicts and form closer bonds where you wish to.

children

The moment you have a child, your relationship with your partner changes irrevocably. Your orbits adjust themselves around the new sun. The mother's bond with her new baby is intensely close and her partner may now seem to be more important as a fellow parent than as a lover. Of course, the proud father loves his new baby but he often misses the exclusive closeness he formerly had with the mother.

Babies change our lives for ever with challenges and joys on all fronts. Suddenly we find ourselves coping with exhaustion, endless chores, no time to ourselves, and a partnership that needs a major effort to keep it from suffering under the strain. At the same time there are deeply precious moments when we look at our new child together with heart-filling love and wonder.

To keep the intimacy with your partner alive while bringing up a baby or toddler, it is important to share in the tasks of parenting in a spirit of mutual empathy. Spend some time every day thinking about the particular stresses your partner is suffering, and take positive steps to alleviate – even to anticipate – them. Make sure that you manage to spend some time alone with your partner, share each other's love and, of course, exchange news and views in the way that you always did. With a little effort you can keep up a strong continuity with your pre-parental selves.

As your child grows, your evolving relationship with him or her can become puzzling or difficult. Learn from other parents about the changes your child is undergoing and establish which issues are individual to your situation. Is your child becoming

distant from you? Does he or she tend to be rude or sullen? Monitor developments closely, and look for explanations. Ask yourself whether you are interacting with your child in the optimum way. Do you come home stressed and keep your child at a distance just to have some peace? How much active time do you spend doing enjoyable things together? Gather an overview of the pattern and see what needs to change.

Being a parent is a difficult job, right into the teenage years and beyond, and we can never get it quite right. The good news is that we don't have to be perfect. All we have to do is to show our love over and over.

friends

Friends are essential to our wellbeing. Good ones can be loyal to us for the rest of our lives, or theirs. A friend provides a space where you can relax and be yourself – even if you are seeing each other again for the first time in years. When our romantic or family relationships go wrong, it is often our best friend that we turn to. Occasionally, that friendship can turn into romance, although this is not the usual turn of events. Perhaps some unspoken taboo is at work, a feeling that it is in some way incestuous to bring physical desire into such a close relationship; perhaps also the cost of failure – the possible loss of the friendship if the physical side of things collapses into embarrassment – is too great to contemplate.

Building a friendship takes skills, which may improve with experience. You start by seeing the potential for friendship in the first place. Perhaps among your acquaintances you feel that someone stands out for some reason. They might have had fascinating experiences, or a talent you would like to learn more about, or they might talk well, in a way that you find really illuminating, or be warm, fun and generally good to be with. If your attraction to this person (there need be no awkwardness in using the term "attraction") stems from what you might learn from them, take the initiative and ask them the questions that intrigue you. There is no need to think of pretext: most people are keen to meet others who are genuinely interested in their lives. If you are drawn to someone because they seem temperamentally suited to you, take a bold initiative by extending some kind

of invitation to them – perhaps involving other people too. If your interest is reciprocated, your friendship will develop by a natural evolution. There will be no need to force the pace, but it would be a pity to neglect any opportunities that present themselves.

Friendships deepen over time if you nurture them well. This requires an investment of time, energy, kindness and honesty. If you are unable to arrange meetings, keep in touch somehow – even a postcard with a one-sentence message can be enough to signal that the friend is in your thoughts. The email is the main thoroughfare of many friendships today, but is this enough? Do you think that your friend might value a letter or a token gift sent via "snail mail" more than a barrage of confessional emails? When trying out new experiences – classes, visits to new places, exhibitions, or perhaps something more unusual and harder to categorize, make a point of asking a friend to try them with you: adventures always gain an extra dimension if they are shared. Alternatively, gather the experiences you have had on your own and shape them in some way to present to your friends. You could perhaps show photographs or tell anecdotes. How much you embellish the bare facts with picturesque detail or humorous flourishes is entirely up to you, but there is one pitfall that is best avoided – boring your friends by spinning out your experiences well past the limits of a reasonable attention span. Do not let your vivid memories of a vacation or fascinating episode at work (to take just two possible topics) drown your curiosity about what has been happening in their own lives.

Don't walk in front of me, I might not follow. Don't walk behind me, I might not lead. Walk beside me and be my friend.

Anonymous

Your task as a friend is to be kind and not to judge any imperfections. This is much easier with a friend than with a love partner, because friends do not usually share a life. The best friendships include admiration of any special gifts the other might possess. If such appreciation is soured a little by envy, try to let go of this as you would any other negative emotion. If you do not feel pleased about your friend's successes, either you disapprove of them in some way or, more likely, there is unacknowledged envy. True friends not only share in each other's happiness, they also instinctively sacrifice personal interests and rush to offer support or comfort whenever it is needed.

Intimate friendships, no less than romantic relationships, are built on trust. And the betrayal of trust can be devastating. Treat the confidences your friends entrust to you with the utmost respect. Above all, do not ever be tempted to tell one friend's secrets to another friend without permission, even if they know and like each other very well. When talking to one friend about another friend, follow this basic rule: imagine the second friend eavesdropping upon the conversation, and choose your subject-matter accordingly; only say what the second friend would be perfectly content to hear you say.

If your partner seems to resent one of your friendships, do not automatically assume that he or she is being unreasonable. Ask yourself if you might be guilty of misplaced priorities, or of using this particular friend as an escape route from any stresses you are experiencing with your loved one. If you suspect this might be so, conversations with both partner and friend are likely to be needed before the situation can be straightened out.

colleagues

Most of us spend a substantial proportion of our lives at work. If the work environment is pleasant and we enjoy our job, this dimension of our experience will feel satisfying and worthwhile. However, for many people difficulties at work make the process of earning a living unpleasant and stressful. This unhappiness can then spill over into all other areas of our lives, corroding our intimate relationships and undermining our health and vitality.

In every work activity there are two aspects: the task and the process. The task is what needs to be done, and when you focus on this you are looking at how to reach a certain goal with a minimum of time and effort. If a work environment is purely task-focused, people feel alienated and exploited.

The process is the human element of the job. When you concentrate on the process, you are asking what the task means both to yourself and to others, and how it impacts on you all. If due consideration is given to process by everyone involved in the task, people feel respected as human beings and they are willing to work harder and for longer hours.

It is vital to make satisfying human connections in the workplace. Delicate issues of status may require you to behave differently with equals, superiors, and people who report to you. However, there are common strands of behaviour that will ease and foster your relations with all colleagues. We all long to be respected and appreciated, and to fully respect someone you have to know the whole person. So listen carefully when colleagues talk about their home life or their interests outside work.

Appreciation is the key to contentment at work. While you may not be able to control whether *you* are appreciated, you can certainly show your appreciation of others. Western society is stingy when it comes to praise. People will readily blame you when something goes wrong, but they will often neglect to applaud you when you perform well. Learn to celebrate colleagues' successes and express your appreciation of them freely. If you treat people with courtesy, appreciation and kindness, you will bring out the best in them. When someone is difficult, remind yourself that only unhappy people turn nasty or aggressive, so try to respond with compassion.

conclusion: where to from here?

Every human being is capable of change. However, change can be difficult because you have to let go of habitual patterns and move into the unknown. Most of us have a tendency to resist change, and it usually takes emotional pain to drive us to seek a different way of being. We must acknowledge that we can change only ourselves, no one else. We can ask our partner, our family or our friends to help us — but this requires us to behave differently toward them, to talk about tricky situations, to risk disagreement. Take time now to review what you have learned from this book, and try to identify what you want to change about the way you interact with your partner and with others.

There are three steps to change. The first is to make the decision to change because you know that there is something wrong; the second is to develop your awareness of what factors precisely are causing the problem; and the third is to implement change by acting on your conclusions. You are already on the road to healing when you realize that change can come only from within. As your determination strengthens, you see that you are locked in a cycle of destructive behaviour. You spend time observing yourself, analyzing what is going wrong. You start to put change into practice, experimenting with your new way of being. You may find yourself drifting back to the way things were. If so, you patiently bring yourself back to your vision again and again until you make measurable progress toward your goals.

To be successful in relationships you must learn to be like a river. Look at how a river deals with obstacles: the water flows

around rocks, finding a new path, never losing sight of its final destiny – to merge with the sea. You can learn from water's gentle strength. Instead of dashing yourself against obstacles, there are ways to flow around the difficulties in a relationship, while remaining true to your own path. No doubt there will be turbulence. In a storm the river rages, carrying branches, even boulders, in its flow. As the flood subsides, the debris will be swept away or dropped on the banks; the waters run clear again. If you can let go of hurt, you will find it easier to make the changes you want. If your life runs true as a result of these changes, you will bring good things to all you meet – not just to your loved ones.

further reading

Aitken, R. *Taking the Path of Zen*, North Point Press (New York), 1982

Bauby, J.-D. *The Divingbell and the Butterfly*, Vintage Books (New York) and Fourth Estate (London), 1998

Beck, C. J. *Everyday Zen*, Harper & Row (San Francisco) and Thorsons (London), 1989

Bradshaw, J. *Creating Love: The Next Great Stage of Growth*, Bantam Books (New York), 1992 and Piatkus (London), 1993

Buzan, T. *The Mind Map® Book – Radiant Thinking*, BBC Books (London), 1993 and Plume (New York), 1996

Dowrick, S. *Intimacy and Solitude*, Reed (Auckland), 1991 and The Women's Press (London), 1993

Dowrick, S. *The Universal Love*, Reed (Auckland), 2000

Goleman, D. *Emotional Intelligence*, Bloomsbury (London) and Bantam Books (New York), 1996

Hanh, Thich Nhat *Teachings on Love*, Parallax Press (Berkeley, US), 1997

Hendrix, H. *Getting the Love You Want: A Guide for Couples*, Schwartz and Wilkinson (Melbourne), 1990 and Pocket Books (New York), 1993

Hendrix, H. *Keeping the Love You Find: A Guide for Singles*, Schwartz and Wilkinson (Melbourne) and Pocket Books (New York), 1993

Hillman, J. *The Soul's Code: In Search of Character and Calling*, Random House (Sydney), 1996 and Bantam Books (London), 1997

Kabat-Zinn, J. *Full Catastrophe Living: Using the Wisdom of Your Body and Mind to Face Stress, Pain, and Illness*, Delta (New York), 1990 and Piatkus (London), 1996

Kirshenbaum, M. *Too Good to Leave, Too Bad to Stay*, Penguin (Harmondsworth, UK), 1996 and Plume (New York), 1997

Kornfield, J. *A Path with Heart: A Guide Through the Perils and Promises of Spiritual Life*, Rider (London), 1988 and Bantam Books (New York),1993

Levine, S. and O. *Embracing the Beloved: Relationship As a Path of Awakening*, Doubleday (New York), 1995

Moore, T. *Care of the Soul: A Guide for Cultivating Depth and Sacredness in Everyday Life*, HarperCollins (New York) and Piatkus (London), 1992

O'Connor, N. *Letting Go with Love: The Grieving Process*, La Mariposa Press (Arizona), 1994

Paget, L. *How to Give Her Absolute Pleasure: Totally Explicit Techniques Every Woman Wants Her Man to Know*, Broadway Books (New York), 2000 and Piatkus (London), 2001

Quilliam, S. *Staying together: From Crisis to Deeper Commitment*, Vermilion (London), 2001

Salzberg, S. *Loving-kindness – The Revolutionary Art of Happiness*, Shambala (Boston and London), 1995

Spring, J. A. *After the Affair: Healing the Pain and Rebuilding Trust When a Partner Has Been Unfaithful*, HarperCollins (New York), 1997

Stewart, W. *Making the Most of Your Relationships*, How To Books (Oxford, UK), 2001

useful addresses

UK
The British Organization for Counselling
1 Regent Place, Rugby
Warwickshire CV21 2PJ
tel: 01788 550899
www.bac.co.uk

The Institute of Family Therapy
24–32 Stephenson Way
London NW1 2HX
tel: 020 7391 9150
www.instituteoffamilytherapy.org.uk

One Plus One Marriage and Partnership Research
The Wells
7–15 Rosebery Avenue
London EC1R 4SP
tel: 020 7841 3660
www.oneplusone.org.uk

Relate
Herbert Gray College
Little Church Street, Rugby
Warwickshire CV21 3AP
tel: 01788 573241
www.relate.org.uk

USA
American Association for Marriage
and Family Therapy
1133 15th Street, NW Suite 300
Washington, DC 20005–2710
tel: 202 452 0109
www.aamft.org

American Counseling Association
5999 Stevenson Avenue
Alexandria, VA 22304–3300
tel: 703 823 9800
www.counseling.org

The Institute for Imago Relationship Therapy
335 North Knowles Avenue
Winter Park, FL 32789
tel: 407 644 3537
www.imagotherapy.com

PREP®: The Prevention & Relationship
Enhancement Program
PREP Inc., PO Box 102530
Denver, CO 80250–2530
tel: 800 366 0166
www.prepinc.com

CANADA
Canadian Counselling Association
116 Albert Street, Suite 702
Ottawa, Ontario K1P 5G3
tel: 613 237 1099
fax: 613 237 9786
email: info@ccacc.ca

AUSTRALIA
Relationships Australia
15 Napier Close, Deakin ACT 2600
PO Box 313, Curtin ACT 2605
tel: 02 6285 4466
www.relationships.com.au

NEW ZEALAND
Relationship Services New Zealand
1st Floor, 1 Robert Street
Ellerslie, Auckland
tel: 0800 735 283
www.relate.org.nz

Wellspring Company
38 Halifax Street, Nelson, New Zealand
www.wellspringcompany.com

index

acknowledgments

AUTHOR'S ACKNOWLEDGMENTS
This book has been shaped by my experience of love and friendship. I thank my past husband, Uwe Grodd, for his gift of a deep and sustaining friendship as a precious outcome of our failed marriage. I am grateful to my partner, David Bagshaw, for bringing passion, playfulness and innocent tenderness into my life. I thank my son, Sebastian Grodd, for teaching me much about integrity and kindness of heart.

A creative adventure, such as this book, needs support and encouragement. I am grateful to my sisterly friends Keeta Davison and Birgit Neumann for cheering me on enthusiastically. Just before cancer cut short her life, Madeline Butler introduced me to Mind Maps®, a creative tool that I have found invaluable. I wrote large sections of this book at Canoe Bay, the most beautiful place on the planet and I am grateful to the King-Turner family for their warm hospitality and long friendship. Finally, I offer my thanks to my editors Ingrid Court-Jones and Judy Barratt who guided me with tact and skill.

PUBLISHER'S ACKNOWLEDGMENTS
The scripture quotations contained herein are from the New Revised Standard Version Bible, copyright © 1989 by the Division of Christian Education of the National Council of the Churches of Christ in the U.S.A., and are used by permission. All rights reserved.

If you would like further information about anything discussed in this book, please contact:
Mary Jaksch
Wellspring Company,
38 Halifax Street
Nelson
New Zealand
email: enquiry@wellspringcompany.com

Mind Maps® is a Registered Trademark of the Buzan Organisation and used with enthusiastic Permission.
Buzan Centres Ltd
54 Parkstone Road
Poole
Dorset
BH15 2PG
UK
tel: 01202 674676
fax: 01202 674776
email: Buzan@Mind-Map.com
www.Mind-Map.com